Sustaining

Extraordinary

Student
Achievement

To teachers and principals everywhere who embrace the noble mission of educating all children to prepare them for a future filled with hope and promise

Sustaining Extraordinary Student Achievement

Linda E. Reksten

CORWIN PRESS
A SAGE Company

For information:

Corwin Press
A SAGE Company
2455 Teller Road
Thousand Oaks,
    California 91320
www.corwinpress.com

SAGE Ltd.
1 Oliver's Yard
55 City Road
London EC1Y 1SP
United Kingdom

SAGE Publications India Pvt. Ltd.
B 1/I 1 Mohan Cooperative
    Industrial Area
Mathura Road, New Delhi 110 044
India

SAGE Asia-Pacific Pte. Ltd.
33 Pekin Street #02-01
Far East Square
Singapore 048763

Printed in the United States of America.

Library of Congress Cataloging-in-Publication Data

Reksten, Linda E.
Sustaining extraordinary student achievement / Linda E. Reksten.
    p. cm.
Includes bibliographical references and index.
ISBN 978-1-4129-1752-0 (cloth) — ISBN 978-1-4129-1753-7 (pbk.)

    1. School improvement programs—California—Case studies. 2. Academic achievement—California—Case studies. I. Title.

LB2822.83.C2R45 2009
371.010973—dc22   2008024371

This book is printed on acid-free paper.

08   09   10   11   12   10   9   8   7   6   5   4   3   2   1

Acquisitions Editor:	Arnis Burvikovs
Associate Editor:	Desirée A. Bartlett
Production Editor:	Jane Haenel
Copy Editor:	Trey Thoelcke
Typesetter:	C&M Digitals (P) Ltd.
Proofreader:	Gail Naron Chalew
Indexer:	Nara Wood
Cover and Graphics Designer:	Karine Hovsepian

Contents

Preface

In the coming year, the number of students needing to achieve proficiency under the No Child Left Behind (NCLB) federal guidelines will dramatically increase not only in California but also across the nation. This will be a wake-up call for "business as usual" schools. It is one thing to look at the number of students across the school scoring proficient and quite another to make sure that every single subgroup is meeting the new proficiency target at the increased level. To make the challenge even more difficult, the number of students scoring proficient will continue to increase steadily along a severe trajectory every subsequent year toward the goal of 100 percent in 2014. Unless schools learn how to sustain and accelerate student achievement for every subgroup, they will not meet each year's increasing target. Additionally, many schools have not had to worry about achieving the Adequate Yearly Progress (AYP) targets but now will be faced with the possibility of becoming a Program Improvement school if they miss the target for every two consecutive years. That target will increase from 35.2 percent in 2008 to 46 percent in 2009 for language arts and from 37 percent in 2008 to 47.5 percent for mathematics. These targets will become a matter of grave concern for almost every school and every school district.

There are, however, Title 1 schools among the most challenged within the state of California, working with English learners and high-poverty children, that have not only achieved but have sustained their student achievement year after year. They have solved their achievement problems and have gone on to improve and sustain achievement for every subgroup. Five such schools are profiled in this book. These schools were forced to change through state-imposed or district-imposed reform efforts. Many such schools facing similar circumstances did not improve. However, these schools learned first how to achieve and then learned how to sustain achievement.

Each school's story is told based on actual interviews and on-site visits. The secrets of their achieving and sustaining practices are revealed within the context of each school's unique culture. Every school was studied from the point of view of the prevailing culture rather than how a district perceived its achievement; that is, the sustaining elements embedded in the culture are not merely cited as a laundry list of effective practices in isolation. These schools are actually implementing these practices, as demonstrated by student achievement scores. Often schools that are trying to improve can articulate elements of sustaining practice but cannot bring about the actual substance of real achievement. School reform can often become relegated to reform du jour or form without substance.

Much of the effective schools' research cited is consistent with the findings of this book. Effective schools research even concurs with much of the sustaining practices reported by this research. Yet, what was uniquely discovered was how the context of these elements works together within the school to produce such outstanding achievement. Research studies often discuss the elements of an effective school but do not focus on how all the elements work together as a whole. Each of the sustaining elements alone will not produce sustaining practice. All must be present within a school's culture.

There is much to learn from each of these schools. Districts, principals, and teachers need to know and understand how to create a high-achieving culture with all essential elements, where everyone is successful—students, teachers, principals, and support staff. Where a low-achieving culture exists and teachers are unsuccessful with student achievement challenges, the school environment becomes caustic and frustrating for everyone. Students or parents are very often blamed for the lack of success. More importantly, low achievement doesn't remain static. It continues to spiral downward, creating more frustration and lower achievement. It then takes a concerted effort to turn around a low-achieving culture to one that is high achieving.

The first task for each of these schools was to build a high-achieving culture. In each case, a crisis triggered the beginning of positive change and leaders emerged from the crisis to facilitate change. At all schools, a set of nonnegotiable core values emerged with a new commitment to high student achievement. Essential elements such as shared leadership, use of data, and strategic intervention were uniquely woven within each culture. The low-achieving mind-set was replaced with a high-achieving culture over time when students began to be successful.

From my own experience in working with teachers to lead Disney Elementary School from an underachieving school to a high-achieving school, I began to wonder how we could sustain the momentum of our student achievement. Disney became an Immediate Intervention Underperforming School in 1999, two years after being named a California Distinguished School. Through this point of crisis, and with the partnership of teachers, parents, and support staff, we grew from an Academic Performance Index (API) of 603 in 1999 to an API of 795 in 2003. It was our goal to be a great school—not merely meet the growth target from year to year.

In the first chapter, the reasons for this study are introduced that led to my investigation of five sustaining elementary schools in California. Sylvan Elementary School, located in the heart of Modesto, is the focus of Chapter 2. This high-mobility school with four different tracks of students learned how to sustain high achievement. Chapter 3 tells the story of Camellia Elementary School, one of the lowest achieving schools in California in the 1970s. Now this school is one of the very highest performing schools in the state. Jefferson Elementary School in Carlsbad is discussed in Chapter 4. Jefferson is noted for its highly collaborative staff, who will do whatever it takes to help students achieve, even if it means working on Saturdays. Rosita Elementary School in Garden Grove (Chapter 5) is an example of a school that continues to sustain student achievement despite four principal changes. Baldwin Elementary School in Alhambra is the focus of Chapter 6. This school is a "triple crown" (California Distinguished School, Title 1 Achieving School, and a National Title 1 Blue Ribbon School) K–8 school that is relentless in helping students to achieve. Finally, Chapter 7 summarizes the findings from the study of all five schools with the essential elements that enable these schools to continue to sustain high achievement.

The principles and practices of these five schools can be replicated in any school. Thus, this is an important book for the professional development of principals and those preparing principals at the university/college levels. Additionally, districts can use this book as a basis for developing in their staffs the understanding of how to create a high-achieving culture to improve student achievement. Then school personnel can see what is needed to sustain and continuously improve that achievement.

It is my hope that principals and teachers everywhere will be inspired and confirmed in their quest to not just simply meet the NCLB student achievement targets but to become truly great sustaining schools year after year. It is important to think beyond just meeting an achievement target to becoming excellent in every way for the sake of the children we serve. These schools provide a pathway and an insight on how to become excellent.

The stories of each of these schools are real and the student achievement is real. I am confident after studying these schools that every school can become a sustaining school. There are no excuses! Embracing sustainability begins with a group of people determined to reject the poor performance of their students and change their practice for the sake of helping their students improve. What are the rewards for taking the risk? For these schools, taking this risk brought the satisfaction and teacher efficacy they now have in seeing their students soar to greater excellence. What a fulfilling legacy for any educator! One of the principals articulated the reward for addressing student achievement well when she said, "When you are successful, it doesn't seem like work." The following pages present the real realities and the exciting results of deciding to be a sustaining school.

Acknowledgments

It was a privilege to capture the stories of these schools so that other schools can benefit. I am grateful first and foremost to the principals for their willingness to be videotaped and/or interviewed to capture the accuracy of each school's culture: Russell Antrocoli, Don Ogden, Mary Marshall, Carol VanVooren, Kathy Roe, Gabriela Mafi, and Liz Hanacek. Second, I want to thank the leadership teams and teachers for their frank input and willingness to talk to a "stranger in their midst." Also, I sincerely thank the support staff that welcomed me into each of the schools and their willingness to share their stories. For many district administrators who contributed to the stories of these schools, thank you for your support. Finally, I am so thankful to the Disney Elementary teachers, support staff, and parents who were willing to work side by side with me to achieve our dream of becoming a sustaining school on behalf of hundreds of children who have benefited.

PUBLISHER'S ACKNOWLEDGMENTS

Corwin Press gratefully acknowledges the contributions of the following individuals:

Lori Grossman
Manager of Mentoring Services
Houston Independent School
   District
Houston, TX

Mary Alice Heuschel
Superintendent
Renton School District
Renton, WA

John Hoyle
Professor
Texas A&M University
College Station, TX

Steve Knobl
Principal
Gulf High School
New Port Richey, FL

Nancy Skerritt
Assistant Superintendent
Tahoma School District
Maple Valley, WA

Fred Wall
Adjunct Professor
Mesa State College
Grand Junction, CO

About the Author

**Linda E. Reksten** has been an educator for twenty-five years: twenty-three years in the public school system and two years as a college professor for Point Loma Nazarene University. A native of Montana, she graduated from Montana State University, Billings, in 1973 with a secondary education degree in biology and chemistry. Immediately after graduating, she went on to earn a master's degree in Christian education from George Fox University in 1976 and served four years as a director of Christian education.

Reksten began her public teaching career in the Burbank Unified School District in 1982 as a middle-school science teacher and high-school chemistry teacher. During the summers, she taught elementary science for gifted students in Grades 4 and 5. While still a teacher, she began her second master's degree at Point Loma Nazarene University, where she graduated in curriculum and administration during the summer of 1985. During 1986, she became principal of Disney Elementary School. Within one year, she began her doctoral studies at UCLA in teaching studies, and she completed her doctorate in June 1995 while she was a principal.

During Reksten's seventeen years as principal, Disney Elementary became a Title 1 school and the most ethnically diverse school in the Burbank Unified School District, with twelve languages and 44 percent of the student population speaking only limited English. Disney became a California Distinguished School in 1997 largely due to the school's technology program. However, through an interesting chain of events, Disney became an underperforming school in 1999. Reksten then took on the challenge of improving student achievement in reading over the next four years. As a result of her leadership and a dedicated, hard-working staff, Disney students' Academic Performance Index (API) grew from 603 to 790 in three years, making it the third-highest performing school in the Burbank Unified School District. Because of this success with students, Reksten and her staff were recognized by President Bush on June 10, 2003, in the White House Rose Garden at the first anniversary of the No Child Left Behind Act.

After serving two years as professor of education at Point Loma Nazarene University, Reksten transitioned back into public education to become the Director of Assessment and Evaluation for Mountain View School District in El Monte responsible for assessment and technology. As of August 2007, she was promoted to Assistant Superintendent of Educational Services for the Mountain View School District, assisting twelve schools to improve their student achievement.

Reksten is the author of *Using Technology to Increase Student Learning*, Corwin Press (2000).

1

Introduction

It is quite a remarkable feat to turn around a failing school, and it is an even more improbable one to continue to sustain and improve student achievement year after year. However, there are schools that are sustaining student achievement in spite of No Child Left Behind (NCLB) or the policy pressure of the hour. How is it then that some schools, regardless of political pressures, sustain student achievement and seem to get better each year? What seems to be the magic formula for these schools? I do believe that the desire to sustain student achievement lives in the heart of every educator. Yet, very few schools are successful and do in fact sustain student achievement.

These questions about sustaining student achievement arose from my own experience of leading the Disney Elementary school community out of a "failure mind-set" to an "achieving mind-set." I recall fellow principals asking me in the midst of the intense work of reversing a failing student achievement pattern, "How can we keep this going?" Sustainability is a perplexing problem faced by every public school, let alone a school forced to improve. The work of sustaining achievement is in fact relentless for, at any time, the pattern of improved student achievement can be reversed. On every front, a sustaining school must continue to persevere through obstacles such as poverty and second-language issues, or it will become mediocre and allow student achievement to slide. It was not good enough for Disney teachers to relax in their pursuit of improving student achievement. These teachers had come too far to settle for becoming just a good school; they wanted to be a great school.

The goal of being a great school had always been in the hearts of the Disney Elementary staff. In 1997, Disney Elementary was recognized as a California Distinguished School. Just two years later, Disney became an underperforming school. The shock of the underperforming label propelled the Disney staff to embark on an improvement process initially forecasted to take three years to exit the "underperforming" status. The initial improvement process instead transformed Disney from underperforming to a sustaining school that continues to sustain achievement as of this writing. As principal, my role was to set the improvement process in motion to exit the state's Immediate Intervention of Underperforming Schools Program (IIUSP). However, this short-term goal turned into a long-term one as the Disney community embraced the notion of being an excellent sustaining school. Even three years after I left my role as Disney principal, student achievement has continued to be sustained.

According to many, Disney broke the "mold" of the high-poverty underachieving school. It became and is to this day one of the highest performing schools in Burbank. From the story of Disney Elementary and my own experience, I began to wonder if the variables that led to our success were the keys to sustaining student achievement at other schools. Are these variables that sustained Disney Elementary the same for other high-poverty, high-achieving elementary schools? These and other questions propelled me into my study of five extraordinary sustaining elementary schools in California. The object of the study was to tell the story of these five schools and identify their key elements that sustained their student achievement.

SELECTION OF FIVE TITLE 1 SCHOOLS

To study why certain schools sustained, I decided to look at high-achieving, Title 1 elementary schools in California similar to Disney Elementary. Additionally, these schools had to have sustained student achievement for a minimum five-year continuous period as demonstrated by the California Academic Performance Index (API), California Standards Test (CST), and federal Adequate Yearly Progress (AYP) data. Selecting just Title 1 elementary schools further narrowed the focus of investigation. If these elementary schools could sustain student achievement in the face of poverty, second-language issues, and a number of other obstacles, the information brought forth could be of real benefit to the field of education.

To identify the top schools, I referenced the Title 1 Achieving Schools state list for specific schools that had sustained student achievement for at least five years. Schools were selected representing both northern and southern California that had sustained achievement so as to give a broad scope of sustaining schools, not just localized to southern California. Each school's record of achievement was rigorously examined to meet the selection criteria.

Variables such as size, mobility, subgroup percentages reflecting English-language learners and socioeconomically disadvantaged were taken into consideration. The schools selected had to have similar challenges and demonstrated sustained student achievement. A few schools initially selected early on in the study were eliminated later because they did not sustain achievement over the course of the study's time frame.

It was further decided that each school would be visited to capture the real story of why these schools were sustaining student achievement. Merely looking at test data or having teachers and the principal complete a survey would not reveal the essence of why that school was sustaining achievement. Thus, a qualitative study with on-site research was selected as the best means to uncover the "story" of the school. Next, each school's principal was contacted for his or her agreement to participate in the study. Additionally, in some cases the district office representing these schools was contacted for permission to participate. Funds for on-site school visitations were obtained through a university grant.

Once each school had agreed to participate, a letter was sent to each principal along with a list of focus areas from which interview questions would be derived. These areas, based on the research on effective schools and my own experience, included (1) developing an achieving culture; (2) empowering staff and parents; (3) standards-based instruction; (4) the use of student data; (5) prescriptive student intervention; and (6) continuous refinement processes. The actual interview questions were not sent ahead of time so that on-site responses would be spontaneous. Schedules for visiting schools were then set with each principal.

In preparation for the visit, an interview guide was developed for the principal and leadership team, with the principal's interview being videotaped. Each principal agreed to be videotaped. In return for the permission to videotape, a DVD record of the interview was created and sent to the principal. The leadership team was interviewed at some schools as a group and individually at other schools, depending on the visitation schedule. It was made clear to the principal that interviewing the leadership team or other staff members separately from the principal was not intended to elicit opposing points of view but to provide clarification and depth for each study area.

Other individuals were also interviewed, especially at schools that had sustained student achievement longer than five years and where the principal and/or key teachers were no longer at that school. Each school's office manager was also interviewed because of his or her important role in managing the school. The office managers also gave me school documents that provided further clarification regarding the culture of the school, such as school policies and the parent handbook. Classrooms were visited, with observations being directed to the study areas. For two schools, a second visit was made to verify key information or obtain more comments from teachers.

FOCUS AREAS FOR STRUCTURED INTERVIEWS

The focus areas were based on research from the California State Board of Education's study of the IIUSP results (1999–2002) and the research of Samuel Casey Carter. According to Carter (2000) in *No Excuses*, there are seven traits of a high-achieving school: (1) excellent leadership; (2) high expectations for ALL students; (3) high-performing teachers; (4) ongoing assessment; (5) improved student discipline; (6) effective parent relationships; and (7) commitment to extraordinary effort by students and staff to achieve outstanding results. Alan Blankstein's (2004) *Failure Is Not an Option: 6 Principles That Guide Student Achievement in High-Performing Schools* further defines principles that undergird the focus areas for this study; namely, (1) common mission, vision, and goals; (2) ensuring achievement for all students; (3) collaborative teaming; (4) using data to guide decision making and continual improvement; (5) active engagement from family and community; and (6) building sustainable leadership capacity. The research derived from the IIUSP helped to illuminate the program execution of each school's IIUSP plan and improved API results. From these and other sources (e.g., Rosenholtz, 1991) of effective schools literature, the following focus areas were selected and are described with sample questions.

1. Developing an Achieving Culture. Establishing an achieving culture in a school where students are not performing is a complex and all-encompassing task. Each school selected had overcome its poor performance inertia to not only improve but to sustain achievement. Each school additionally had developed an achieving culture formed from the beliefs, practices, and principles that set student achievement as the highest priority within the school community. Two questions asked of principals and leadership teams about their achieving culture were "What were the most important steps in establishing this culture?" and "What are your nonnegotiable core values?"

2. Empowering the Right People. To create a sustaining school, these schools needed to relentlessly pursue improving student achievement. Early in the development process, it would be the case that not everyone was "on the same page" with this objective. A question such as "How were the leadership team, teachers, and classified staff empowered?" was critical to revealing the various roles that the principal, teachers, and classified staff took in the improvement process. According to Neuman and Simmons (2000), effective school leadership is no longer viewed as a function of age, position, or job title, but shared by all. Another question asked of principals and teachers was "How did you work with reluctant staff?" It was vital to understand how each school dealt with reluctant teachers when it was creating a shared leadership structure.

3. Standards-Based Instruction. High-performing schools have high-performing teachers. These teachers are excellent in their instruction and also work effectively in grade-level teams or departments. However, they typically don't start out that way. It was critical to determine what made the difference in transitioning to quality coordinated instruction with every teacher taking responsibility for student learning. In probing this issue, the following questions were posed: "What processes are in place that monitor how students are mastering state standards?" and "How is student data used to affect ongoing instruction?"

4. Use of Student Data. Ongoing assessment should be another characteristic of these high-performing schools. Effective schools research contends that frequent assessment of all students during the year is the best way to determine if every child is learning according to the second edition of the Consortium on Reading Excellence reading sourcebook (Diamond, 2007). Consequently, putting a coordinated system of assessment in place is an important transition schools must achieve. Questions such as "How did you put a system of assessments in place?" and "How do teachers use student assessment data?" were intended to search out in detail how the school developed its own internal accountability system.

5. Prescriptive Student Intervention. Response to Intervention (RTI), a new requirement in the 2004 Individuals with Disabilities Education Act (IDEA), contends that intervening with struggling students early is essential to improving their achievement. At each selected school, student deficits must be addressed through intervention. Again, a shift in the culture of the school must occur to establish student intervention processes. Both principals and teachers were asked, "How do you identify struggling students?" and "What is the role of the principal, leadership team, and teachers in intervening with struggling students?"

6. Persevering Through Refinement. In *No Excuses*, Carter (2000) contends that extraordinary effort will yield extraordinary student achievement results. He documents this conclusion through the successful schools he has profiled across the United States. It is so impressive that each selected school did sustain student achievement for five years or more. However, sustaining achievement does not occur by happenstance. Identifying the important processes and attitudes that created sustaining practice was critical. Questions such as "What are your key processes in sustaining student achievement?" and "How is staff continuously motivated to persevere toward improvement?" sought to describe each school's motivation to continue to pursue higher and higher student achievement.

THE FIVE SUSTAINING SCHOOLS

The story will be told of five remarkable schools that are getting the job done year after year. These schools are true success stories, stories that are not being told on the political front pages of education publications. Each school consists of heroes and heroines who every day make a difference in the lives of their students. We have much to learn from these schools: Sylvan Elementary School, Camellia Elementary School, Jefferson Elementary School, Rosita Elementary School, and Martha Baldwin Elementary School. This book is an effort to tell the whole story of sustaining practice. For the teachers and principals of these schools, sustaining practice consists of making their students successful.

1. *Sylvan Elementary School* is a Title 1 school located in Modesto, an urban agricultural setting in central California. Student mobility is high, and Sylvan is the first to receive students and the first to relocate students and teachers to new schools due to growing enrollment within the district. To add to its challenges, the school has four educational tracks running continuously. Sylvan additionally faces the challenges of poverty and English-language learners.

2. *Camellia Elementary School* was known as a "school out of control" in the early 1970s, with its performance scores at the very bottom of all schools in California. Located in the Sacramento area, Camellia is now one of the highest performing Title 1 schools in California and the United States with literally no achievement gaps between any subgroup populations. Parents wait in line to get their children into this school.

3. *Jefferson Elementary School,* located in Carlsbad, on first glance looks like a private school. However, this school is a Title 1 school where a large percentage of students come from poverty and are English-language learners. In this school, teachers are known for their collaboration and work ethic even beyond the school day.

4. *Rosita Elementary School,* located in Garden Grove, is a Title 1 school with 70 percent first-generation immigrant Americans from Mexico, and the remaining 30 percent of the students are from Vietnam. Of all the schools studied, this school has the highest number of English-language learners. Yet, this school is sustaining achievement in spite of principal changes. The district office plays a dominant role in helping to maintain a structure that sustains student achievement.

5. *Martha Baldwin Elementary School* is a rare "triple crown" school in Alhambra, having received Title 1 Achieving School in 2002, 2003, 2004, 2005, 2006, and 2007; California Distinguished School in 2002, 2004, and 2006; and National Blue Ribbon School in 2003. These accolades are rare for a K–8 elementary school also dealing with middle-school students. However, this school is relentless in continuing to improve student achievement.

In the following chapters, the stories of each of these schools, which were derived from data analyses of the visits, observations, and interviews, are told. One chapter is dedicated to each school. Every school's story is told in depth to illuminate the sustaining elements that make each of these schools successful. Further, beyond the analysis of the sustaining elements these schools have in common, the story of how each school uniquely addresses sustaining achievement is analyzed. The final chapter presents a discussion of the findings and recommendations for other schools that seek to become successful sustaining schools.

2

Sylvan Elementary School, Modesto, California

A Culture of Effective Instruction

Located in the heart of Modesto's unique urban residential/ agricultural setting, Sylvan Elementary is the flagship school of now ten schools in the Sylvan Union School District. Sylvan is a "home" to 535 children who come and go on four different tracks due to space constraints in an aging school structure. Sylvan teachers address the academic needs of and provide a "family" for a student population comprised of 41 percent Latino, 40 percent white, 7 percent African American, 6 percent Asian, and small percentages of other cultures. Of this group, 19 percent are English-language learners, and 54 percent are socioeconomically disadvantaged (SED) learners. "This school has always felt like family," several teachers commented. The school dog—"Buddy"— certainly contributes to the family atmosphere that permeates Sylvan. Because of this family atmosphere, a majority of teachers have sent their own children to Sylvan. "It is not for the convenience of sending our children here but because we truly love what we have accomplished on this campus," said one teacher.

> ### Buddy, Sylvan's School Mascot
>
> Buddy, who belongs to one of the longest tenured teachers, has become a central figure at this school. Every day Buddy signs in with a paw print made for him. He gives awards such as Buddy's Buddies, a citizenship award. Buddy is best known for his "Buddysburg Address," a video of Buddy (with a voice-over) making a speech about STAR testing to motivate students.

Sylvan is an "overflow" school, housing students for relocation to newly constructed schools. District enrollment is growing as families flee from the San Francisco and San Jose areas to secure more affordable housing. This accounts for the 35 percent mobility at Sylvan as both teachers and students are sent to "birth" new schools. Throughout all the movement of staff and students, there remains a core group of teachers who are respected in Modesto. These teachers are known in the community and take great pride in nurturing and preparing students, as well as new teachers, to fit in and become successful at Sylvan. A genuine spirit of fun and laughter pervades Sylvan. It is not uncommon for teachers of all grade levels to meet and share lunch together and to see the latest movie filmed by students. In the face of all of the daunting challenges related to mobility and four separate school tracks, it is remarkable that this school has sustained its student achievement goals for the past five years.

Sylvan Elementary School is one of a select group of California Title 1 schools that has achieved what others would call impossible. For more than five years, Sylvan students have substantively increased student achievement as shown by California's Academic Performance Index (API) and the Adequate Yearly Progress (AYP) federal No Child Left Behind (NCLB) measures. Table 2.1 shows the impressive achievement pattern over the past five years. Note that for five years, Sylvan students have defied the odds, achieving much more than expected for the Latino and socioeconomically disadvantaged subgroups, as compared to other schools like it that are making very little progress. Table 2.1 further identifies that, in the year 2000, the school dropped in student achievement. It was at this point of very low morale in 2001 that Sylvan's new principal, Russell Antracoli, entered the doors of Sylvan and led the staff to reclaim its pride and dignity, all the while propelling the staff and students toward higher and higher student achievement. This success did not happen by accident but through a set of sustaining elements that were meticulously put into place for this kind of achievement to be realized.

BUILDING A HIGH-ACHIEVING CULTURE

Building a high-achieving culture of effective instruction at any school is a difficult task that resides with the leader, the principal, whose chief role is

Table 2.1   API Scores for Sylvan Elementary School

Year	1999	2000	2001	2002	2003	2004	2005	Seven-Year Growth
Schoolwide API	655	626	658	727	745	794	790	135
Latino Subgroup API	596	576	643	707	730	765	790	194
White Subgroup API	676	641	668	743	770	833	821	145
SED API	603	586	613	679	705	747	752	149

that of facilitator. He or she must make an honest assessment of the organization—what is working well and what is not. He or she must begin first with morale building by listening to staff and highlighting their positive contributions and then addressing changes that need to occur next. The principal must initiate clear communication channels in the school to frame the goal or vision for the work of the school and build consensus toward a course of action. The goal must always be about believing that all students can achieve and then showing teachers how to make that happen with their instruction. This is what occurred at Sylvan over the period of five years.

When Sylvan School dropped in student achievement during the 1999–2000 school year, the high esteem in which the school was held for so many years was severely diminished. Prior to the drop in student achievement, Sylvan was administered for two years by a principal who did not fit with the culture of the school. The office manager said things were so stressful that "she had a heart attack at the counter helping a parent." Staff morale was very low because "we didn't have a goal or purpose."

The staff was mortified at an all-district meeting where awards were given out to schools and Sylvan Elementary School was not given any awards. Worse yet, Sylvan was given the "Challenge Award" because its API scores went down. What was intended to be helpful to the Sylvan staff proved to be very hurtful. Needless to say, the staff was humiliated. Even today, the scars are still there when the incident comes up in conversations with teachers. Out of this hurt rose, as Antracoli put it, the "initial motivation for change and the commitment to raise student achievement." When school staffs come to a crossroads of intense pain from real or perceived failure, they choose one of two directions—they either make a commitment to dramatically improve or they permit themselves to fail further.

When I first met Antracoli, I found him to be unassuming and humble. There is a genuine kindness about him, and you sense from the way he talks that he cares deeply for the staff and students. In our initial interview, he was quick to give credit to the staff and others around him. He expressed concern that my visit, though important to the school, not disrupt the classroom instruction because rarely does he miss interaction with the students during recess. Constantly he is out on campus making daily classroom visits.

Teachers and support staff consistently commented on the principal's leadership. It is so apparent that this principal sees his role as the instructional leader. Every staff member in my interview praised him to the utmost. "He is a cheerleader. He got everybody on an even playing field and kept reminding us the way we needed to go." One of the most important actions a principal takes is providing direction and articulating clear steps toward a given goal. Treating everyone with the same respect and appreciation helps staff to come together and to minimize division. "He lets us know when we are doing something well," referring to his personal comments and notes in the bulletin about excellent teaching. "He works very hard and is always coming up with new ideas and new programs to help our kids." Like any good principal, he is proactive, always seeking solutions to problems and programs that work to help students. "Russ is amazing and the most effective principal I have ever seen."

"Russell has it all memorized in his head," the office manager told me. Many stated that he is constantly on the go and has incredible follow-through on details. Sylvan teachers saw that this principal valued their teaching and that he was willing to work hard with them to reclaim their status as a successful school. It is unusual to find a staff with so much regard for their principal. Essentially, the staff's perception of principal effectiveness is due to the fact that Antracoli was discerning enough to deal with morale issues first by recognizing good teaching and then setting a course to improve classroom instruction.

When a principal arrives at a new school, it is imperative that he or she discern the culture of the school quickly. Antracoli spent considerable time identifying several important factors requisite to reclaiming and extending a culture of student achievement. First of all, he didn't make any changes right away, but first observed and then built staff morale and communication. A new principal's first task is to build rapport and trust with all staff. In such a context of trust, teachers can be led to take action to solve problems. To build morale, "I highlighted the positive; I went into the classrooms and saw teachers teach. I publicly acknowledged good teaching through notes, through bulletins, and through staff meetings. I let teachers know that I had confidence in them and I thought they were good teachers," Antracoli said.

Several teachers stated that, within the first few months after Antracoli arrived, all the teachers began to feel better about their work. Emphasis on the positive helped everyone to work toward solutions. This was clearly evident in that in the principal's very first year Sylvan regained the API points it had lost. Next, Antracoli had to establish credibility with teachers, which he did by his willingness to work as hard as they did on behalf of the school. He also gained credibility with teachers by his understanding of good instruction, having taught for twenty-two years.

Developing a Culture of Instruction

Very often teachers are given a data "shock treatment" to show how "bad" the student achievement scores are, a negative, hapless approach that doesn't help the teachers understand how they can raise scores through good instruction. Antracoli's analysis did not look at individual student data but instead looked at what students had to know to take the California Standards Tests (CST). It wasn't just a review in general terms on the standards but rather an analysis of performance on the essential standards. He identified two types of standards: (1) foundational ones in which students can't learn other skills until that standard is mastered (e.g., third-grade multiplication tables) and (2) those standards frequently assessed (e.g., multiplication with regrouping on the CST) for which students would be held accountable.

Improving the teacher's delivery of instruction is very often the key to improving student achievement, so there must be a defined process outlined for that delivery. Sylvan grounded its process in the work of Madeline Hunter, especially her direct instruction lesson format. Antracoli was fully aware of the need to create such a process: "You can have every teacher in your school understand what the essential standards are and you can have good standards-based instructional materials, but if you don't have good instruction and know how to deliver the instruction, that's not going to work."

Madeline Hunter (2004) maintains that lessons must be planned based on teacher decisions that include the content of instruction and the learning behavior of students. The initial decision of what should be taught is determined by what students already know and what is next to be learned in the curriculum that forms the basis of an instructional objective, which guides the entire lesson development. Once the objective is identified, teachers arrange the content and skills for students to learn and how these will be presented to students, which Hunter terms "input." Lesson input usually includes (1) an anticipatory set to initially focus students on the learning and (2) modeling directly the content and skills to be mastered. Student learning behavior, termed "output," is elicited through (1) checking the understanding of students through signals (e.g., thumbs up/down), choral responses, or questions directed to the entire class during modeling; (2) guided practice where all students practice correctly under the watchful eye of the teacher; and (3) independent practice where students practice new learning without the teacher, either seat work or homework.

Often teachers make a leap from modeling to independent practice without guiding students through enough practice to master the content or skill. Incorporating guided practice after modeling allows the teacher to see if students have an initial understanding of the learning. Without guided practice, students end up working on their own, practicing errors, and learning independently without the teacher. Correct application of Hunter's lesson design gave rise to Sylvan's instructional philosophy: "We strongly believe there is no independent practice before it is time and that guided practice, whether it is structured or semistructured, is the most important part of any lesson."

> "We strongly believe there is no independent practice before it is time and that guided practice, whether it is structured or semistructured, is the most important part of any lesson."

Efficient Use of Time

The efficient use of time is a tenet of Hunter's model. Instructional time spent on engaging *all* students rather than a few students is a more productive use of class time and enables all students to practice the new learning. With the emphasis on guided practice (practice while the teacher watches) instead of independent practice (homework or seat work), more time for instruction is redeemed so that more of the curriculum can be taught and mastered. The principal cited as an example a fourth-grade lesson on long division during the first week of the unit. He observed the teacher complete several sample problems with all students participating in guided practice. The teacher didn't ask students to do any independent problems at the end of the lesson. In the conference, Antracoli asked her why she didn't assess the students at the end of the lesson. She said, "It was the first two days of long division. They can't do long division yet. Why give them something they would fail on or make mistakes on? I'll assess them when *they think* they can do it." Antracoli said, "It made perfect sense to me and we now have a philosophy of no independent practice before it is time."

Another example had to do with reading comprehension. To see if students can use inference, teachers don't need to give students twenty-five comprehension questions. They can check to see if the children can use inference with three questions. "Good teaching is not giving a lot of work; good teaching is teaching the kids and assessing them with very little time, and that saves the teacher time. They don't have to spend the day grading papers. You can spend your whole day teaching."

> "Good teaching is not giving a lot of work; good teaching is teaching the kids and assessing them with very little time, and that saves the teacher time. They don't have to spend the day grading papers. You can spend your whole day teaching."

By insisting on Hunter's lesson format, the principal systematically developed a common language for effective instruction that transformed the prior instructional culture. Second, the efficient use of instructional time was reclaimed. Turning assessment of students into an everyday activity resulted in teachers not wasting so much energy on grading numerous homework tasks.

SYLVAN'S NONNEGOTIABLE CORE VALUES

Every school has a set of core values. These values, whether positive or negative, form an unwritten genetic code that determines the motivation or lack thereof of staff. It is the job of the principal to reclaim and reorient staff toward the positive values the staff holds as professional educators. Prior to Antracoli's arrival, a pattern of negative values had clouded the teachers' and support staff's purpose as educators. To reclaim the positive values that were buried beneath the negatives, the principal constantly reminded the staff, "We first of all teach children; we focus on children," thereby shifting the focus from the painful circumstances of failure to teaching the students today. Next the staff as a group identified three guiding principles or nonnegotiable core values:

1. *High expectations* for all students, teachers, and the principal.

2. *No excuses!* As educators we do not place blame or find excuses for not achieving success. We must teach this to our students also.

3. *Ownership!* The students in our classes are our responsibility for the year. We must look to our instruction as the key element in student success. Yes, interventions will come, but we are the key element in student achievement.

These values were agreed to within three months of the principal's arrival. "It was easy to create this because teachers were willing to accept it. We really believe in these things." He emphasized that these principles were always there—the staff just didn't know they were there. These values are articulated throughout the school among teachers, staff, and students.

Reorienting teachers to have and maintain high expectations for students—especially low-performing students—is imperative for student achievement to improve. Teachers must deliberately and consistently teach to high goals for all students to improve. In schools that are low performing, teachers are sometimes unaware of their own lowered expectations for students. These low expectations must be confronted (usually by the principal) so that teachers begin believing that low-performing students can achieve. Because this transformation took place at Sylvan, students who would be viewed as low-achieving students today are achieving more than higher achieving students were ten years ago, due to elevated student expectations.

One of the most important actions of the principal is to vigorously fan the flames of high expectations for all students. Students, teachers, and staff need to be reminded frequently because the work is hard and demanding. At Sylvan, such occurs in an effective and nonthreatening manner. Occasionally if the principal sees the belief wavering, all he does is make copies of these guiding principles and puts them in the teachers' boxes as a little reminder that this is what Sylvan teachers really believe in. These values are also articulated frequently to the students. Students must have the message that the teachers, the principal, and the staff expect a great deal from them. "If we correct the students," Antracoli said, "they may say, 'It wasn't my fault,' and we say, 'There are *no excuses*. We know you can. We have high expectations for you and we know you can do this.'" These clearly and frequently articulated core values, woven into the fabric of learning and personal behavior lived out by the principal, teachers, and staff, do affect students immeasurably.

EMPOWERING STAFF TO DO THEIR BEST WORK

To empower teachers, the principal must "get on the same page" as the teachers. The fact that this principal in the first year formed a bond with the Sylvan leadership team was an important piece of empowering Sylvan's teachers. Often principals will disconnect themselves and their work from their teachers and/or come into schools with their own agenda. They take on their shoulders the entire weight of changing the school. So, principals get caught up in the mind-set of having to always be the expert rather than looking for experts on their staff.

First of all, the Sylvan teachers became empowered because the principal paid close attention to the effect of the "Challenge School" label, which had crushed staff pride because of their prior record as a high student achievement school. Most of the teachers stated, "We needed direction, and Russ turned everything around by helping everyone focus on the same goals." When staff feel that they have had a voice and have been heard, they are prepared to move forward. When principals come in with an agenda and fail to listen to staff, they essentially create a recipe for their own demise. Sylvan's principal knew that it was the principal who must build leadership in the staff to create a sustaining organization. Principals must see their role as one of support to teachers and other staff rather than as one of overshadowing staff. The staff's gifts and talents associated with leadership must be nurtured and developed.

Another aspect of empowering was the principal's unwavering belief that successful organizations just don't have one leader and he or she is at the top; they have leaders throughout the organization that stimulate change and initiate new ideas. As a strategy to identify leaders within the staff, the principal structures faculty meetings and grade-level meetings. The leadership of teachers is cultivated at these meetings where teachers collaborate and grade-level leaders conduct the meetings. The principal tries to limit the number of meetings where he "bores" them to death with details. "We allow them to do collaboration and talk about good teaching and share what's working with other teachers." This structure enables teachers to have a voice and to assume responsibility for the plans associated with improving student learning.

The Sylvan leadership team, comprised of one teacher per grade level, selected by the grade level, played a very important role during the principal's first year and his successive years as principal. Members of the team went with the principal to workshops on school improvement at the Stanislaus County Office of Education that first year and helped to make a significant number of important decisions. For example, the daily intervention structure, the plan for after-school intervention programs, and the choices for materials to be used in interventions all were devised by the principal and the leadership team. A spring "Leadership Day," a full-day meeting, was set aside to monitor the progress of new program changes. The second year, the leadership team met to revise the intervention structure, decreasing the number of days but increasing the minutes per day. They again met in the spring and planned for the next year by adding a math intervention and changed the way supplemental teachers were scheduled. Overall, the team and the principal forged a positive working relationship during this time that later served as the model for how the grade-level teams were to function.

For each spring leadership team meeting, the principal asks each grade level to identify a representative to attend this meeting. Release time is given for the grade-level representatives. Antracoli then develops the agenda, outlines important information on specific issues, and provides the general outline for teachers to review in grade-level meetings prior to the leadership team meeting. After giving a brief overview of the issues on the day of the meeting, Antracoli then leaves the meeting. "I like to give them

> "I like to give them ownership to change. It works better that way."

ownership to change. It works better that way." Teachers then work with the instructional facilitator to come up with solutions that are given to the principal. Where Antracoli disagrees with one of the solutions, he meets with the leadership team to negotiate consensus on a course of action.

Very few principals would leave a leadership team meeting and allow the team to solve schoolwide issues. Many principals prefer to control the results of these meetings or would have previously determined the course of action prior to the meeting where team attendance is merely symbolic. This principal really expects his team to own the changes. The leadership team also meets three to four times after school throughout the year to discuss concerns such as playground supervision, assemblies, and the like. A grade-level representative is in attendance; however, any teacher can sit in on these meetings. Leadership team members, in turn, lead grade-level meetings to plan and implement curriculum, analyze data from assessments, score student writing, and deal with other issues as needed.

Members of the leadership team play a critical role in the hiring of new teachers. Present at the interviews are the grade-level leader, one parent, and at least one classified staff person from the Sylvan staff. Sylvan Union School District usually hires a pool of teachers via a representative district committee from which schools can interview teacher candidates when openings occur. By involving the grade-level representative in the hiring process, ownership and mentoring for the new teacher are set in place for that grade level because he or she had a voice in hiring.

Part of Sylvan's success, I am convinced, is the principal's strongly held belief that he must give staff all the credit for the good work done with the students. He believes that if the teachers succeed with students, it's the teachers who deserve all the credit, and when students don't succeed, it's the principal who accepts all the blame. Teachers praised the principal for how effectively he buffers them from parent issues, criticisms, "touchy situations," and other pressures. It is rare that the principal accepts the total responsibility for the performance of teachers, staff, and students. Very often principals will blame others for poor performance to deflect attention from themselves and their role. Blaming sets up an adversarial position, whereas accepting the blame gives staff no other recourse other than to continue to perform better.

Providing support to teachers is another role that some principals fail to value. Principals who define themselves solely by "being in charge" will rarely empower teachers to become effective in their instruction with students because such a principal is too busy focusing on his or her own responsibilities. Antracoli had it right when he said, "Principals are support personnel. Anyone who is not a teacher is a support person. Sometimes school leaders tend to forget that. They tend to forget they support classroom instruction." His unflinching support of teachers won the hearts of his teachers. Sylvan teachers I interviewed verified the support they felt from the principal. In the lunch "inner sanctum," they spoke frankly about Antracoli. Teachers candidly told me that Russell "knows when to leave people alone" and "he trusts us and lets teachers teach their own way as long as we are going (in the same direction) together."

> "Principals are support personnel. Anyone who is not a teacher is a support person. Sometimes school leaders tend to forget that. They tend to forget they support classroom instruction."

They put forth a great deal of effort to ensure that I understood the difference between the lack of support from the prior principal and that received from Antracoli. They further corroborated that "he never puts you out and he takes the blame for teachers. He buffers the teachers really well." He also is quick to ask teachers what they need and follows through as soon as possible. Above all, teachers stated that Antracoli deeply cares what they care most about—their students. "He has a deep heart and loves all kids. He knows all kids can learn and makes everybody else care." It is obvious that when principals selflessly support teachers, giving them all the credit, providing clarity of purpose and direction, the teaching staff will continually challenge themselves to become even better teachers.

Keeping the "Right" People

A school cannot be successful without a coordinated staff effort. Very often one can have a great vision for a school but not have the right staff to get it done. Another critical role of the principal is to work with the teachers and support staff to help them refocus on becoming successful or, in the alternative, help them leave the school. Now, working with staff is not for the faint-hearted or for those without people skills. In the beginning, it is a tough job to evaluate staff on achievement issues and systematically confront those issues with individual teachers. But it must be done. Once the right people are in place, the collaborative efforts of all lead to student achievement improvement.

Sylvan is faced with the challenge of being an overflow school for students in the district due to rising enrollment. During the principal's second year at Sylvan, half of the students and half of the teachers were to leave when a new school was opened. Because Sylvan would be losing half of its students and some teachers right away, Antracoli set up a careful balance between the teachers who would leave and those who would stay. Those who were experienced, who were essential to the culture, and who had experienced Sylvan's difficult years would stay to become part of the solution here. Teachers with

> Now, working with staff is not for the faint-hearted or for those without people skills.

mid-range experience and those who were relatively new were transferred. "A lot of times a principal might say that's a good way to get rid of the people you don't want. I didn't choose to do that. I would rather work with people."

Again this decision is an unusual one for principals. Typically the weakest teachers are transferred so that principals won't have to work with low-performing teachers who could jeopardize student achievement. In schools where the transfer of teachers may not occur, principals at times choose to tolerate low-performing teachers within their staff and wonder why students don't perform. Antracoli has had experience with putting the instructional program first and recommending the firing of a teacher. "The first time I made a choice to not reelect a teacher, I didn't tell anyone (as it is confidential). It wasn't a teacher I hired. You cannot believe the teachers on the staff that thanked me for doing that. Teachers knew that it was right for this person."

I have found that teachers usually know who the weak staff members are. When the principal has the courage to confront and even go so far as to recommend termination for a teacher who is performing poorly, respect on the part of the staff—teachers and support alike—increases significantly.

Reluctant Staff

The principal's best approach to dealing with reluctant staff is to establish rapport with them, not ignore them. Principals must find something these teachers are really good at and positively highlight that within the school, especially for those teachers who are negative. For example, one of the Sylvan teachers who does not prefer the new Houghton Mifflin state-adopted reading series makes negative statements at every opportunity; however, the principal thinks she is a wonderful person, loves kids, and does many good things for the school. "When I have conversations with her about the reading series, it is always between her and me and *never* with other people in the room. I also always emphasize publicly all the great things she does for the school." It would be wise for every principal to discuss differences in private and extol reluctant teachers publicly. Often, the principal can become caught in a disagreement with a teacher that may affect other staff within earshot, creating an even bigger problem.

Another strategy for reluctant teachers is to "get out of their way," especially when they are getting results with the students. For instance, one teacher's instructional approach was generally contrary to Sylvan's preferred methods. After three months on the job, Antracoli came to realize this teacher embodied Sylvan's core values and got results, and kids learned. "She has never referred a kid for special education—*ever*! She likes taking those kids below grade level and gets them to where they need to be. So my attitude is to get out of her way."

New-to-Sylvan Teachers

Sylvan teachers see their principal actively working with new teachers as one of his and the school's strengths, primarily because of the focus on the instructional process and classroom effectiveness. New teachers meet with Antracoli at least once a month. The instructional facilitator and other Beginning Teacher Support and Assessment (BTSA) program teachers at the school also assist new teachers. I am convinced that helping new teachers become effective in the classroom is one of the best strategies for improving student achievement. Supporting new teachers in their instructional process is the wisest approach to improving and sustaining student achievement.

Evaluating the Principal's Effectiveness

This past year, Sylvan staff members were asked to evaluate Antracoli by way of an anonymous survey to provide the principal with input on his performance. Typically when the staff identifies areas for change, Antracoli changes his behavior. Recently the staff survey gave him feedback on perceptions of his work behavior. "They were right that sometimes I acted like I was the only one who had anything to do and it was good to get that information." He changed his behavior. Allowing staff to give the principal feedback says to teachers that the principal is accountable as much as they are. Additionally, when the principal acts on staff feedback, it helps teachers to focus on the positive work of their students rather than to continue with complaints about the principal—complaints that will distract teachers from their most important work—instruction.

USING STUDENT DATA TO GUIDE CURRICULUM AND INSTRUCTION

Pinpointing assessment data is fundamental to improving student achievement. In schools where students are not achieving, there is either limited understanding of the value of data or the inability to translate the meaning of the data into quality instruction. Schools that are not sustaining achievement often lack a coordinated system of data collection and analysis by the principal and the leadership team. The principal must purposefully direct the instructional program based on what the data show as targeted weaknesses in student achievement. Improving the instruction in these areas of weaknesses is critical to sustaining student achievement from year to year.

> In schools where students are not achieving, there is either limited understanding of the value of data or the inability to translate the meaning of the data into quality instruction.

Data provided through California's STAR testing system—California Standards Tests (CSTs) and California Achievement Tests, version 6 (CAT/6)—as well as curricular assessments are used to provide information for both curriculum and instruction at Sylvan. During the summer, the principal analyzes the CSTs and the CAT/6 administered to students during April and May. Antracoli looks first at the areas of weakness within the language arts and mathematics tests. "I can tell you right now that we have been weak on writing conventions, so that is an area we have continually targeted, and it has been a focus of our after-school programs this year. Our fourth- and fifth-grade math scores have not been as high as our second- and third-grade math scores. So one of the things I have done is made sure that my fourth- and fifth-grade teachers I have hired are strong in math." The Sylvan staff does not look at isolated skills, for example multiplying a two-digit number by a four-digit number with regrouping. Teachers target weak areas and make those the focus of their instruction. Looking at weak areas in the STAR data by grade levels is an excellent way of looking at weaknesses without risking blaming any one teacher. Data can be presented to teachers in such a negative way that teachers become demoralized and could not care less about improving anything. A wise principal will shape the data presentation in terms of grade-level weaknesses with a plan to address them without casting blame.

The other way that data are used is to target the CST scaled scores of individual students to identify how close each student is to the cut-off scores for Advanced, Proficient, Basic, Below Basic, and Far Below Basic designations. Sylvan looks at the number of children in each area. The teacher's goal is not to move students from the Far Below Basic level to the Advanced Level but rather to move them to the next level and maintain that. Students just below the Proficient level receive interventions. Such an intervention allows every teacher to concentrate instruction on four or five students who may be close to the next level. Targeting the Basic students is a practical means of improving schoolwide performance because these students can easily move up to that all-important Proficient or Advanced level, satisfying the Annual Measurable Objectives (AMO) targets set forth in the AYP report.

What is being used at Sylvan even more than state testing data to drive instruction are the new pacing calendars established for language arts and mathematics. Organizing the curriculum to strategically emphasize key standards and systematically address each student during the year is fundamental to preparing students for greater achievement. Antracoli explained that one of the reasons that Sylvan's test scores were not as good in fourth- and fifth-grade math was that teachers were not finishing the state-mandated curriculum. "I tell my teachers that it doesn't matter that you had to spend more time on this concept or you didn't get to these concepts; it is going to be on STAR and it is not fair that our kids have not had exposure to these concepts." Antracoli commented that there are eight questions on negative and positive integers on the fifth-grade test in the last chapter of the textbook. "If you don't get to that chapter, those same questions are still going to be on that test." To show achievement gains on the CSTs, students must be exposed to essential curriculum and essential standards.

To monitor language arts this year, Sylvan uses the Reading First Theme Assessments (from Sacramento Unified School District) that are closely aligned to the California Language Arts Standards. Although not directly related to the Houghton Mifflin program, these assessments provide individual student information on fluency rates, comprehension, skills check, spelling, and vocabulary. The assessments are very challenging for the principal and teachers alike. Assessments are collected from every teacher, and Antracoli completes a school analysis for every grade level, looking for relative weaknesses and strengths, then makes suggestions for instructional program changes. Teachers review this analysis in grade-level meetings and make adjustments to their curriculum and instructional program. For example, to increase the fluency rate of students, the second-grade teachers decided to spend the first ten minutes of each Universal Access intervention period working on fluency practice. Universal Access is a forty-five minute, in-school intervention period at the end of language arts core instruction where students are differentiated based on reading skill.

Also based on the Reading First Assessments, teachers introduce vocabulary with greater depth in what they describe as "Four Block." Students learn antonyms, synonyms, multiple meanings, and context clues with vocabulary associated with Houghton Mifflin stories. "This way of introducing vocabulary helps to put students into the mind-set of how they will be assessed on STAR," the principal stated. Additionally, the comprehension sections are difficult, providing students practice in inferential reasoning and other forms of complex thinking. This outside source of assessment, not directly related to the language arts curriculum, tells Sylvan teachers the extent to which students are mastering the key standards. It is especially helpful that students are reading "cold" text not based on the material in Houghton Mifflin. This creates a real testing situation every six weeks that is very similar to STAR.

Teachers originally wanted to use the Reading First Assessments for student grades but worked with Antracoli to make some accommodations for grading. For example, some teachers are using the fluency measure within the Reading First Assessments for 25 percent of the students' grades. Teachers, however, primarily use the Houghton Mifflin assessments for grading and help students to set goals for fluency based on the results of the Reading First benchmarks. Teachers also use the Reading First Assessments to reteach and reassess areas of

> "The best assessment bar none is the ongoing daily assessment that the teachers do every single day during whole-group and guided-practice instruction."

weakness. This year, teachers are targeting skills check and fluency—areas they saw were weak in the STAR assessment. Still Antracoli maintains, "The best assessment bar none is the ongoing daily assessment that the teachers do every single day during whole-group and guided-practice instruction." Antracoli is right about that. The following summarizes Sylvan's key principles for using data in instruction.

Sylvan's Principles for Using Data in Instruction

1. Identify relative weaknesses and strengths within the STAR data when planning instruction.

2. Identify individual students in their different performance levels (Advanced, Proficient, Basic, Below Basic, Far Below Basic) within STAR. Focus on the Basic students for the intervention programs. For Far Below Basic and Below Basic students, efforts should be to raise them from Far Below Basic to Below Basic to Basic.

3. Schoolwide assessments that are used to monitor curriculum and instruction will help the teacher's instructional program to consistently improve. The data the teacher sees from his or her instruction are the most important.

4. Sylvan's mantra: Don't overassess because, if you assess too much, you eliminate teaching.

Taken together, as well as in separate pieces, current assessment data are so powerful because they show where students are achieving at specific points during the school year. The ability of teachers to analyze student data results and then to use that data to make timely adjustments in their instruction is essential to improving student achievement schoolwide.

ONGOING IMPROVEMENT OF INSTRUCTION

Sylvan implements a very clearly defined model for teacher observation of classroom instruction. The observation model adapted from Madeline Hunter's effective teaching model includes Daily Review, Demonstration/Modeling of New Material, Guided Practice, Feedback/Corrections During Practice, and Additional Comments. The principal uses this format extensively for teacher observation and creating dialogue about teaching. On this form, he will highlight and analyze the elements of the lesson and then conference with teachers. This model shown in Figure 2.1 is used with all teachers and has served to build a "language of instruction" with teachers.

Because Antracoli was adamant that all the teachers be trained in this model, every teacher now stresses these elements in the classroom. "Effective teaching is the one thing the teachers and I have control over. We must do it right." Occasionally, if a Sylvan veteran teacher sees this

> "Effective teaching is the one thing the teachers and I have control over. We must do it right."

observation model as silly, the principal responds, "Effective teaching is the most important thing we do. My job is to help you improve, even if you are already good." Each year new teachers and teachers scheduled for evaluation

Figure 2.1   Informal Observation/Coaching Session Form

Teacher:	Observer:	Date:
Lesson Type:	Lesson Length:	

Daily Review (F D NF)	**Demonstration/Modeling** (F D NF)
(Review/reteach difficult skills, strategies, or ideas from previous day's/week's lesson.)	(Provide an overview/introduction and set purpose. Introduce new skill(s) clearly, one thought at a time. Ensure mastery of each step before moving on. Give many examples & a few non-examples. Overteach difficult points. Use questions to monitor student progress.)
Guided Practice (F D NF)	**Feedback/Corrections w/ Practice** (F D NF)
(Ask fact and process questions. Demonstrate think-alouds for high-level questions. Prompt responses and fade teacher prompts as mastery occurs. Give additional process explanations and repeat main points. Check until student responses are firm. Provide many choral, partner, and written response opportunities.)	(Corrections are immediate and appropriate. Reteach when errors occur. Feedback is positive and efficient. A 90% accuracy rate is maintained.)
Independent Work (F D NF)	**Additional Comments:**
(Direct students through first few problems. Actively monitor students. Keep interactions short, but frequent.)	
F – Skill is firmly in place.	**D – Skill is developing.** **NF – Skill is not firm.**

Source: Adapted from Stanislaus County Office of Education's Consortium of Underperforming Schools materials.

are oriented to this model. Also addressed in teacher conferences are the California Standards for the Teaching Profession. These standards are primarily used for initial teacher credentialing and for BTSA support of probationary teachers at schools. Use of both the Hunter model and the California Standards for the Teaching Profession has standardized the instructional process for teachers. Observation feedback given by the principal serves the purpose of clarifying the instructional process by reflecting on strengths, challenges, and areas of weakness.

A set of *Core Elements of Instruction* presented by Leslie McPeak (2000), from Stanislaus County Office of Education to the Consortium of Underperforming Schools is a second model Sylvan has adapted to help teachers become effective in their instruction, as well as to orchestrate the instruction of teachers across the school.

Instruction is guided by a preplanned curriculum. All curricular areas now at Sylvan have standards-based curriculum and pacing calendars that have been established for language arts and math. Pacing calendars provide a blueprint for specific standard emphases.

Teachers have high expectations for students. Though difficult to observe, expectation levels become evident in ongoing assessment analysis at grade-level meetings.

Students are carefully oriented to lessons. Orientation to lessons refers to providing students a clear objective of what they are to learn during the lesson. Sylvan students must know what they are supposed to be able to do at the end of the lesson.

Instruction is clear and targeted. Clarity within lessons usually stems from a clear instructional objective followed by input/modeling and guided practice aligned with that objective. For instance, if the lesson is on triangles, classifying triangles and finding the missing angle are all the lesson is to be about.

Learning progress is monitored closely. As students practice, teachers must be moving about the classroom, ensuring that students are practicing correctly. Sylvan teachers know they will get a note from the principal should he walk into a classroom where students are working at their seats but the teacher is in the back of the room grading papers. The veteran teachers are quick to tell the new teachers, "This is what Russ doesn't like."

Students are retaught, as necessary. Usually, students don't understand the learning the first time around. Often teachers try to teach too much within a lesson time frame. Teaching reverts to a covering of information rather than helping students develop any kind of mastery. Reteaching at times is necessary to solidify new learning and develop mastery. New teachers at Sylvan often try to teach too much information without helping students develop mastery. Antracoli assists new teachers in correcting this kind of instructional error by helping them listen to student answers for correctness before teaching the next curricular objective.

Class time is used for learning. Class time is not for busywork. Busywork is characterized as work unrelated to any learning objective or work that does not challenge students. Class time is to be dedicated to instruction and practicing new skills associated with grade-level goals.

Standards for classroom behavior are explicit. Explicit standards for student behavior are critical to learning. Without order in the classroom, students cannot learn. Sylvan teachers are committed to the fact that when students are either off task, not at work, or not listening, they need to have direct and explicit standards to redirect students back to the activity. The purpose of this is to maximize teaching and learning time.

There are smooth, efficient classroom routines. Effective routines occur when the instructional focus changes and movements from whole-group to small-group tasks or transitioning from one activity to another takes very little time. Sylvan is dedicated to this proposition: The better the routines and procedures, and the better students know and use them, the more the teaching time will be available.

Instructional groups fit instructional needs. Whole groups and small grouping of students in the classroom must benefit all students, not only those at grade level but also those below grade level and above grade level. During whole-group lessons, the emphasis is especially on getting the struggling students involved through a variety of interaction strategies. It is critical to engage students through echo, choral, partner reading, and other forms of interaction. These strategies keep all students alert and engaged and do not let the lesson interaction be reduced to just those who voluntarily respond and the teacher.

Student-teacher interactions are positive. The teacher-student interaction must always be positive and encouraging to students. Encouragement and praise that motivate students should be quick and to the point, allowing the lesson to continue at a good pace. In a hostile classroom, students are reluctant to participate or fearful.

Incentives/rewards are used to promote excellence. Students must be given recognition for their accomplishments in the classroom and schoolwide. These awards are important motivators for students to keep working hard. For example, Sylvan recognizes accomplishments such as 250 sight words in first grade, multiplication facts through 12 in third grade, and fluency levels for each grade as well as Citizenship, Honor Roll, and STAR achievement awards. Recognition encourages students to continue to reach the high expectations the principal and teachers believe they can achieve.

In summary, these elements are used for standardizing instruction and developing a common language for instruction across the school. They also provide clarity to teachers regarding what is expected in working with students.

STRATEGIC INTERVENTION WITH STUDENTS

Sylvan has a number of ways to deliver strategic intervention. The first method is through daily classroom instruction. After a lesson has been

taught that includes guided practice and some assessment, teachers identify students who are ready for independent practice and others who are
not. Students who need more guided practice meet with the teacher in the
back of the room for reinforcement and reteaching, if necessary.

A second strategic approach is through "cooperatives." Twice each
year, the resource specialist (RSP) teacher, the principal, learning facilitator, and school psychologist meet with every teacher and review every
student in need of intervention. The first line of defense is Sylvan's
Universal Access Reading Group, a planned grade-level intervention conducted during the morning at the end of the language arts period, and
secondly, the after-school intervention program. Between the time of the
cooperative meeting and the next cooperative meeting, teachers apply
interventions to identified individual students. During the second cooperative, assessment data are reviewed for each child identified in the first
cooperative. Teachers look at "how those kids are doing, and identify the
ones who are not improving and ask why? What aren't we doing that we
should do?" A special group that is always carefully monitored between
the cooperatives is made up of students who have been retained. If by
October of the current school year (the school year begins in July) retained
students are not making progress, teachers identify different strategies to
intervene with those students.

One of the most tactical interventions at Sylvan is the Universal Access
period that occurs within the school day. This period is organized by grade
level (Grades 1–5) and staffed by designated teachers and specialists:
English Language Development, Resource Specialist, Title 1, and supple-
mentary teachers from other school tracks designated as Universal Access
teachers. This period is scheduled four days each week, Tuesday through
Friday. Groups of students are differentiated based on reading needs.
Some students work independently during this period also. For example,
during a forty-minute fifth-grade Universal Access, students can be found
practicing reading fluency with a reading passage, engaged in paired reading and summary paragraph shrinking (PALS), part of a group meeting
with a teacher completing a story map, or part of a group working on a
summary writing project. Across the week, students will have met in all of
the differentiated types of groups to build reading skills. Special education
students meet with the Resource Specialist teacher during this time as well
so that they are not pulled from the core instruction during the day.

Many schools typically intervene by pulling out students from the
classroom. Sylvan is very passionate about not doing this, believing that
all students need to be exposed to the core curriculum, whether or not
they are ready for the core curriculum. The principal insists that students
in special programs not be pulled out from the regular classroom during
core instruction time during the day. "When I first arrived, ten or twelve
students would be pulled out during core instruction time. These
kids are going to be taking STAR and they have to be there for core

instruction." The year he arrived, he had seventeen students testing at a lower grade level on STAR in the Special Education Program. Currently no students are testing out of level. "This is not high expectations when students test out of level because they are all going to have to take the STAR test," he said. Some may disagree with Antracoli on this and make excuses for special needs students. However, the performance record of special needs students is fraught with those who have not improved in achievement.

> … all students need to be exposed to the core curriculum, whether or not they are ready for the core curriculum.

Sylvan uses a variety of after-school intervention programs that are based on the STAR areas of weakness as well as the ongoing Reading First Assessment analysis of individual students. The classes are multilevel but each student has an assessment diagnosis. The class size is not more than fifteen students with a teacher and an instructional assistant. The class is scheduled during the afternoons three days per week for one hour. Some of the interventions are as follows.

- **Reading Fluency Lab.** Most of the students in the reading fluency lab are second- and third-graders using the Read Naturally program. During the regular school day, teachers use "adaptive Read Naturally" in classrooms applying the fluency strategies to the story summaries in the Houghton Mifflin Reading Program.
- **Reading Comprehension Lab.** The SRA Reading kits are used in this after-school intervention to build specific skills and multiple skills in reading comprehension. Generally, Sylvan uses programs that are easy to use for teachers and don't add to their preparation time.
- **Math Problem-Solving Lab.** This lab helps students gain proficiency in the types of math problems that will be presented on the STAR tests
- **Writing Conventions Labs.** Two grade-level groups (Grade 2/3 and Grade 4/5) address the weaknesses identified on last year's STAR assessment and the Reading First Benchmark Assessments.
- **Intercession Classes.** There are both math and reading intercession classes. Both are scheduled during the mornings at the end of each of the four school tracks. Preference is given to Grade 4 and 5 students with some Grade 3 students. The reading intercession program consists of SRA Reading comprehension, Read Naturally fluency practice, writing conventions, and scripted lessons from Fontana Unified School District's Program, Focus on Achievement. The Rewards Program, used for fourth-graders, is a six-week program developed by Anita Archer focusing on multisyllabic decoding in content area reading. This program is continued and finished in the afterschool

program after the two-week reading intercession program ends. Two math intercession classes target math enrichment and math remediation. The math enrichment concentrates on hands-on algebra. The math remediation is based on diagnosed weaknesses of students. For example, for fourth- and fifth-graders, the weaknesses usually are in division, multiplication, and problem solving.

SYLVAN'S SUSTAINING ELEMENTS

The most important sustaining elements and practices at Sylvan identified by both the principal and teachers are the following.

- **A Positive Atmosphere for Success.** Both the principal and teachers are committed to the belief that all students can be successful. Teachers are ever willing to work very hard to help students. The principal is the school "cheerleader," constantly encouraging and building the staff morale. He is a highly skilled instructional specialist who consistently shares with teachers how instruction makes a difference in student achievement. He is vigilant in spending the time necessary to support students, staff, and parents. As one teacher explained, "Russ is scary amazing! He pushes us hard and supports you no matter what."
- **Emphasis on Good Instruction.** Teachers have developed a culture of instruction where elements of lessons are standardized. They have become reflective practitioners, and they are encouraged to always take the next step. Teachers also understand that student assessment data provide critical feedback on student learning. They have learned to translate that data back into more improved instruction. Finally they have learned from Antracoli that, "It is important what you teach and what you use to teach, but the most important factor is how you teach."

> "It is important what you teach and what you use to teach, but the most important factor is how you teach."

- **Staff Pride in Raising Student Achievement.** After meeting the Sylvan staff, I was struck by how proud everyone is of their school and how grateful all are that Antracoli had helped them regain their dignity and pride. The Sylvan atmosphere is charged with the positive energy of a staff that is successful and knows why they are successful. It is this pride that drives teachers to continue to improve student achievement.

Overall, Sylvan has become a school in which the students are constantly achieving, the staff is successful, and the parents are proud to send their children there. In spite of the challenges, lack of space, four tracks, being an overflow school, high poverty, and mobility due to rising enrollment, Sylvan is excelling because of its insistence on quality instruction with students. More than five years of sustained student achievement are testimony to this success. Most likely, the school will meet an API of 800 this year in California. Sylvan is no longer a school needing to be challenged but a school that is getting the job done in California and showing the way for other schools to become better.

LESSONS LEARNED FROM SYLVAN ELEMENTARY SCHOOL

Put an Unrelenting Focus on Classroom Instruction to Improve Student Achievement. Teachers all use a common language of instruction based on Madeline Hunter's model of effective teaching. This targeted instructional model is applied universally in every classroom. The principal and senior teachers assist new teachers with instruction and planning.

Buffer and Support Teachers in Their Important Task of Instructing. The principal sees himself as "support personnel," with his chief function that of helping teachers be successful instructors with students. He handles all parent issues and any issues that distract teachers from their main job of teaching students. He accepts the total responsibility for the performance of teachers, staff, and students. Teachers commented that this principal "trusted them and allowed them to teach their own way as long as they got results with students."

"We strongly believe there is no independent practice before it is time and that guided practice, whether it is structured or semistructured, is the most important part of any lesson."

3

Camellia Elementary School, Sacramento, California

A Culture of Order and Discipline

Tucked away in a rural section of southeast Sacramento is one of the highest performing Title 1 schools in California, Camellia Basic Elementary School. This school is also in the prestigious top 10 percent of highest performing schools in California. As I walked up Camellia's long walkway on a rainy January morning, the school appeared from the exterior as a typical California elementary school with the normal bustling of children being dropped off by parents at the beginning of the school day. Approaching the double-door entrance, I could hear the kindergarten teachers and children singing as they entered the classroom exactly at 8:00 AM. Entering the school foyer, I was immediately taken by the trophy cases of plaques, letters from prominent legislators, and pictures celebrating the many awards this school has received. Even with the wet rainy conditions that day, I was surprised at the cleanliness of the foyer, cafeteria, and office areas. You could literally eat off the floors. Across the foyer in the cafeteria, banners were hung prominently from

Table 3.1   API Scores for Camellia Elementary School

Year	1999	2000	2001	2002	2003	2004	2005	Seven-Year Growth
Schoolwide API	814	847	860	842	878	873	901	87
Asian Subgroup API	834	848	860	827	867	871	895	61
Latino Subgroup API	814	855	847	847	865	864	897	83
White Subgroup API	817	854	894	889	922	924		107
African-American Subgroup API	761	816	832		869			108
SED API		838	853	838	870	865	895	57

the ceiling accentuating the success and pride teachers, staff, and students must have in this school—California Distinguished School for 2002 and 2006; Exemplary School by Sacramento City Unified School District in 2000, 2001, and 2002; Governor's Performance Award for 2002 and 2004; Magnet School of Merit; California Title 1 Achieving School in 2002, 2003, 2004, 2005, and 2006; and No Child Left Behind National Title 1 Blue Ribbon School in 2003. The accomplishments of this school were shouting from the walls.

For the past thirty years, Camellia students have exhibited a pattern of sustaining student achievement. In 1999, when the API was first calculated for schools in California, Camellia had already exceeded the governor's 800 goal in all but one subgroup—African American, with 761. The very next year, the African American students exceeded the 800 API benchmark and did not go below 800 again for any subsequent year. They were a very significant subgroup. The Latino, Asian, and socioeconomically disadvantaged (SED) subgroups have never dipped below 800 and have continuously improved over the years. The gaps so prevalent in schools between white, African American, Latino, and SED students are nonexistent at Camellia. Students have consistently demonstrated outstanding student achievement, as shown in Table 3.1.

The success that so characterizes Camellia today was not the case thirty years ago. Camellia in the early 1970s was a very difficult place to work. The school drew students from an all-black, poor neighborhood. With a 99 percent "segregated" black student population, the NAACP brought a lawsuit against Sacramento City School District in 1975. Even before the NAACP legal problems, Camellia was known as a school "out of control" with many student fights that fostered an ongoing climate of chaos. In 1972–1973, Camellia also bore the title of the lowest achieving school in Sacramento City and the second lowest achieving school in California. Frank Meder, a former teacher at Camellia, recalled that the average student was performing below the 10th percentile on the California Test of Basic Skills (CTBS) given in California at that time. Due to this reputation, Camellia could never keep teachers or principals. Teacher turnover was more than 50 percent each year. Consequently, only new teachers and interns were sent to Camellia (some of these original teachers and interns are still at Camellia today). Experienced teachers in Sacramento City School District who were aware of Camellia's problems shunned the school. As a result of these and other problems, a cloud of despair hung over Camellia, so common to an underperforming school.

DEVELOPING A CULTURE OF ORDER AND DISCIPLINE

In response to the NAACP lawsuit, the Sacramento City Board of Education made Camellia a "basic school" to attract other ethnicities. However, the Board did not consult or collaborate with teachers about this decision. They read about the result the following morning in the newspaper. This pronouncement left teachers sorely frustrated because they had started to change the student behavior that made working at the school so unbearable. They now felt coerced into creating this new school concept. However, the decision to become a basic school proved to be a blessing in disguise.

Beginning Steps to a High-Achieving Culture

"We knew what we wanted," stated Mary Marshall, the principal when Camellia was made a basic school, who immediately began working with teachers to establish the initial principles that still frame the fabric of the school culture today. Teachers rather than the principal developed these tenets. The foundational principle already in process was to develop a culture of discipline and order. Even prior to the lawsuit settlement in 1980, and without the direction of a principal, teachers had made great strides in addressing schoolwide discipline.

Frank Meder, one of seven rookie teachers in the 1970s, led the way by establishing "classroom meetings" in sixth grade. Sixth grade was a key grade level because most of the student fights occurred there. As a new teacher still taking university classes, he learned about classroom meetings, a management philosophy espoused by Rudolph Dreikurs (Dreikurs & Cassell, 1991) in his work *Discipline Without Tears*. Frank began using classroom meetings to set out logical consequences for behavior during the 1974–1975 school year. He had so much success with improving student behavior that other Camellia teachers began to notice. The kind of classroom meeting that Frank held was not a meeting to simply share information with students about the class or school. Camellia's classroom meetings provided students with the opportunity to participate in a group exchange of ideas to solve conflicts and encourage personal responsibility and peer accountability in an atmosphere that is respectful and caring.

Toward the end of that year, several teachers came to Frank for training in this effective student management method. By the next school year, most of the teachers were implementing classroom meetings and collaborating extensively with each other. There was unified implementation because the climate of the school was so difficult that teachers were willing to try anything that worked. One kindergarten teacher labeled this a "no-risk philosophy" in that "it couldn't be worse than it was." As teachers became successful in managing students and addressing key reading issues, student achievement scores improved in the late 1970s.

With Camellia's reputation of being the second lowest achieving school in California, Camellia teachers also assumed responsibility for the learning issues—specifically reading. They used the inventory tests from the Ginn Reading Series to identify where students were performing. Not a single student in Frank Meder's sixth-grade class could read past the second-grade level. This was especially alarming for Frank and other intermediate teachers. To attack this problem, teachers put students in grade-appropriate reading materials. For Frank's sixth-grade students, second-grade materials were given to the students. "I put students in the second-grade books where they could read the materials. When they finished the second-grade materials, I went on to the third-grade materials." Other teachers followed what Frank did. Camellia teachers decided to assess students twice during the year to check the progress of student learning. In the late 1970s, student achievement was improving along with schoolwide behavior.

Some teachers who did not buy into the new practices of classroom meetings and the reading assessment focus left the school. The prevailing pattern had been to leave as soon as possible due to Camellia's reputation of being a terrible school. However, what began to emerge was a core of teachers who were unified and empowered in managing student behavior and curriculum and instruction decisions. Other teachers coming into the school had to assume responsibility especially for student behavior in the same way as the core staff or they left the school. One teacher commented,

"The inappropriate staff was weeded out." This unified group of teachers assumed total responsibility for the management of student behavior as well as curriculum and instruction issues schoolwide. They developed a core belief that if they worked together, they could make great things happen

> They developed a core belief that if they worked together, they could make great things happen for kids—whether or not they received any help from anyone to do it.

for kids—whether or not they received any help from anyone to do it. It is important to grasp that 100 percent of Camellia's teachers were unified in this belief. This unity became the second basic tenet of Camellia's culture.

Developing a Basic School

Other important principles that helped to build Camellia's achieving culture came as teachers and the principal developed a basic school in 1980. Teachers had no idea what a basic school was. So, they visited other basic schools in Sacramento City School District to gather ideas. The concept of "basic school" was the same as "magnet school" in Sacramento. Frank Meder recalled that when visiting other basic schools, he and his colleagues didn't see the same kind of interaction with kids that had begun to develop at Camellia and he did not see "real teaching." He remembers observing students working quietly, completing worksheets instead of seeing teachers interacting with the students. Camellia teachers felt that interacting with students was paramount, due to their classroom meeting structure and the direct explicit instruction they had begun using with students. Evaluations made from these visits to Sacramento's basic schools helped to shape teacher decisions of what *not* to do in their basic school.

Camellia's principal remembers the great opportunity they had to develop a kind of school different from a regular school, and Mary Marshall is fondly remembered by Camellia teachers as someone who really empowered them. She was wise in allowing teachers to take responsibility for Camellia. In her own words, "I have always been a teacher-principal. I have always thought of myself in the mix—not in a line of command, and so

> "I have always been a teacher-principal. I have always thought of myself in the mix—not in a line of command, and so I never separated myself from my staff."

I never separated myself from my staff." Frank recalls her as someone who really supported teachers, even at times when the teacher was at fault. She is credited with enabling teachers to set academic and behavior standards, establishing a study center, and eating lunch with students, which is the practice even today at Camellia.

Marshall also was instrumental in working with teachers to establish an academic plan. Camellia teachers could now do things differently from a traditional school. One of the early concerns was having enough time for teaching—especially reading. In a traditional setting with a practice known as *divided opening,* very little time was spent on academic learning. Much time was spent monitoring two different arrivals and two different dismissals of students, leaving little time for instruction. She remembers with satisfaction that a schedule was established where one full hour each was given to reading, mathematics, and language every morning. Teachers could finally concentrate on reading! During the afternoons, teachers became specialists in a subject area and departmentalized science, history/social science, music, art, and P.E. For example, one teacher would be responsible for teaching Grades 4–6 sciences. Additionally the practice of *looping,* especially in the intermediate grades, was initiated. Looping is a practice where teachers follow a class of students across two grades. Since teachers already knew the learning styles and achievement patterns of their students, they could begin immediately instructing students at the next grade level, thereby losing no time.

Along with an academic plan, emphasis in the early days of developing a basic school focused on good first instruction and high expectations. Instruction was interactive and explicit from teachers to students, and this continues to be emphasized today at Camellia. The question, "What did you teach the first time?" is a question that teachers often ask themselves and others when analyzing learning or behavior challenges.

> The question, "What did you teach the first time?" is a question that teachers often ask themselves and others when analyzing learning or behavior challenges. It is a cultural reminder at Camellia to stress the importance of the "first teaching" students receive.

It is a cultural reminder at Camellia to stress the importance of the "first teaching" students receive. In the beginning, when students were performing poorly, the plan was to strategically address their academic performance level and then gradually teach to higher expectations and beyond. All teachers share this viewpoint. One kindergarten teacher said that she shuns the comment, "Oh, they are just kindergarten students" when parents or others question the capabilities of her students. All teachers expect their students to achieve at Camellia at a very high level, and they will not permit others, including parents, teachers, or the principal, to think otherwise.

Additional practices adopted for a basic school included the following.

A Parent Application Process. To attend Camellia School, parents had to submit an application. The application was not solely based on achievement or language proficiency but on core agreements. Additionally, parents needed to get their names on Camellia's list. In later years, parents often camped out overnight to claim the few spots available for the coming school year. Even today there is a waiting list.

Three-Way Learning Contracts. Every teacher, child, and parent at the beginning of the school year sign Camellia's contract. Agreements are made for academic achievement, attendance, citizenship, homework, and a parental commitment of forty hours of volunteer time that must be given to Camellia during the school year. Working parents are willing to give this time because they want their children to go to Camellia. Students must adhere to only missing three days of school, going to bed by 9:00 PM, regularly completing homework with support from parents, and other requirements. If parents and students do not abide by the guidelines, the student forfeits his or her right to attend Camellia. This three-way learning contract is represented in Figure 3.1.

Basic Means Basic. The curriculum at Camellia is basic, with a focus on reading, language, and mathematics as a first priority in the mornings. Instruction is delivered directly and explicitly to students. Assessment is used to check student learning and provide instructional focus. Curriculum is paced and orchestrated by grade levels uniformly and monitored by the teachers. When new teachers arrive at Camellia, a member of the core group of teachers will take that teacher aside and say, "This is how we teach reading at Camellia."

> When new teachers arrive at Camellia, a member of the core group of teachers will take that teacher aside and say, "This is how we teach reading at Camellia."

THE RIGHT STAFF STAYS AT THE SCHOOL

There is no doubt that the "basic school" concept that resulted from a lawsuit back in the 1970s assisted the development of an achieving culture at Camellia. However, beneath the basic-school structure is a highly successful core group of teachers who have remained at Camellia for years, providing continuity and promoting the successful teaching practice that has resulted in a sustaining pattern of outstanding student achievement. These teachers have given many years of their lives to sustain Camellia as a high-performing school: "No matter who comes in as principal, no matter what Board of Education is there or superintendent, they are not going to let their school go down," stated the principal, Don Ogden. One of the newer sixth-grade teachers reverently added, "This is the house that Frank, Ada, Ridge, Sue, and Nancy built," indicating the respect she has for these veteran teachers.

> "No matter who comes in as principal, no matter what Board of Education is there or superintendent, they are not going to let their school go down," stated the principal, Don Ogden.

Figure 3.1 Camellia Basic School Three-Way Learning Contract

Student	Parent	Teacher
Academic Achievement 1. I will do the best work at all times. 2. I will take advantage of every opportunity to learn. 3. I will have in class the necessary tools for learning. 4. I will complete assigned work neatly, accurately, and on time.	**Academic Achievement** 1. I will encourage and support my child's efforts to learn. 2. I will maintain contact with the school and my child's teacher(s). 3. I will review my child's progress with his or her teacher. 4. I will seek help from the school when needed.	**Academic Achievement** 1. I will encourage each student to do his or her best work. 2. I will serve as a good example through my enthusiasm for teaching and learning. 3. I will evaluate student progress and report to each student and parent at regular intervals. 4. I will have a written grading policy that is available to students and parents at the beginning of the year.
Attendance 1. I will go to school every day unless I am ill. 2. I will go to bed by 8:00 PM (Primary), 9:00 PM (Intermediate).	**Attendance** 1. I will assume responsibility for the regular attendance of my child. 2. I will get my child to bed by 8:00 PM (Primary), 9:00 PM (Intermediate). 3. I will drop off and pick up my child(ren) on time. 4. I will have my child at school by the time the morning bell rings at 8:00 AM.	**Attendance** 1. I will motivate good attendance through high-quality instruction, incentives, and positive communication with students.
Citizenship 1. I will know and follow district, school, and classroom rules.	**Citizenship** 1. I will know and support district and classroom rules for acceptable behavior.	**Citizenship** 1. I will have written classroom rules and will discuss them with parents at Back

Figure 3.1 (Continued)

Student	Parent	Teacher
2. I will respect the rights of others at all times. 3. I will follow the dress code and wear the school uniform.	2. I will teach my child to respect the rights and property of others at all times. 3. I will send my child to school with instructions to pay attention in class anc to be respectful. 4. I will assume responsibility that my child follows the dress code and wears a school uniform.	to School Night and with students on the first day of school. 2. I will endorse all rules fairly and firmly. 3. I will maintain an attractive and well-managed classroom, conducive to good student behavior and learning.
Homework 1. I will set aside time after school each day to review what I have learned. 2. I will complete (neatly, accurately, and on time) the assigned homework. 3. I will not cheat on work or tests.	**Homework** 1. I will provide a quiet time and place for study without television. 2. I will know the school's homework policy.	**Homework** 1. I will provide homework designed to reinforce what has been taught in class. 2. I will provide students and parents with written information about the homework policy in my class.
Parent Involvement Our family will contribute 40 hours of volunteer time to the school and its programs. We understand that if we do not, our child(ren) will be disenrolled at the end of this school year. Sixth graders whose families do not complete the 40 hours will not be recommended for the middle school basic program or any school through open enrollment.		
Signature of student Date	Signature of parent Date	Signature of teacher Date

This core group of teachers does not fit the pattern of senior staff that can be found at many other schools. Often, veteran teachers are not as productive in their later years of teaching. At Camellia, even though these teachers are old enough to retire, they are highly successful with students and take great pride in shaping newer teachers to shoulder the mantle of Camellia's achieving culture. "The success they feel here goes beyond salary and any other issue," stated Ogden. This veteran staff is continuously improving their teaching and deliberately models for newer teachers what it takes to get the job done with students. Some teachers even drive long distances to remain at Camellia. "In this school, the talented teachers stay teaching."

Camellia's Hiring Policy

This core group has also established a schoolwide philosophy that teachers coming into Camellia must remain and retire as teachers. This philosophy is foremost in Camellia's hiring policy. "We don't want someone who wants to be a teacher for three years and then be a principal. We want people who are going to come in here and work until they retire and not let all their hard work disappear. We want teachers who will make it their life's ambition to make this a great school and do whatever it takes," Ogden said. This philosophy is not usually found at Title 1 schools where turnover is commonplace for both teachers and principals.

> "We don't want someone who wants to be a teacher for three years and then be a principal. We want people who are going to come in here and work until they retire and not let all their hard work disappear. We want teachers who will make it their life's ambition to make this a great school and do whatever it takes," Ogden said.

As principal of Camellia for eight years, Ogden has preserved and enhanced Camellia's achieving culture by hiring staff with this same philosophy. He has fought the placement of inappropriate staff and works with teachers to select those who plan to remain at Camellia. "I don't give personnel a soft place to land if teachers aren't doing the job somewhere else. We've had some staff leave and I stopped some staff from being placed here," stated Ogden.

This principal also feels that it is his responsibility to deal with teachers who are not performing. "When someone is not doing their job, it is my responsibility to do something about it." Ogden is convinced that when he has addressed the poor performance of teachers, in the long run he has received support from the core teachers. He also believes that it is his responsibility to help teachers who are not effective to become effective. "Every principal has to learn to read his or her staff and ask what do I need to do to make this teacher the best teacher they can be. It is all about the art of being a principal."

USING STUDENT DATA TO GUIDE CURRICULUM AND INSTRUCTION

When Ogden arrived at Camellia several years ago, he helped teachers to become even more effective with students. Ogden wisely valued and respected the high-achieving culture that had been established by Camellia's core teachers and propelled them from an API of 814 to 896 today. Improving student achievement was consistent with their core values. "Camellia teachers were uniform on discipline but independent contractors on curriculum," stated Ogden. He started at the beginning of the school year by meeting with grade levels to review student test scores broken down in a variety of ways, by quartile and by curriculum strand. "The goal back then was to get every student over the 50th percentile first." Every student was discussed by name, with his or her scores broken down by quartile. The performance of each class was also reviewed by strand.

Ogden remembers discussing with teachers the curriculum alignment with the California Standards and STAR Test. At that time, there was not a standards-based language arts curriculum in California and teachers were using a variety of materials. Ogden's first task with teachers was the adoption of a new standards-based language arts curriculum. The staff selected Open Court and with Title 1 funds brought in two reading coaches (one for primary and one for intermediate grade levels) to assist with implementation and coordination of this new curriculum. The focus for teachers was to determine what concepts and skills students needed to know to perform well on the standardized test.

The second year, Ogden again met with teachers at the beginning of the school year to review student test data. This time, they focused on math achievement. They looked at the math standards and where there were deficits in student learning, and they selected the standards-based Saxon Mathematics Program. The second year they not only looked at how students had

> "Here is where the students are performing. Now what are we going to do about it?"

achieved the previous year but also at the students coming into each class in the grade level. The question Ogden posed to teachers was, "Here is where the students are performing. Now what are we going to do about it?" The third year, Ogden worked with teachers to address writing, since Open Court didn't have a strong writing program. Ogden's strategy was to strengthen one program each year. A staff development workshop was arranged, followed by a two-day retreat during which teachers developed Camellia's writing program to coordinate with Open Court.

Grade-Level Assessments

Ogden made a significant change in that third year by arbitrarily shifting seven teachers to different grade levels to put together more cohesive and stronger grade-level teams. He also staffed every classroom with an instructional assistant. This was a significant move that might have defeated another principal, but Ogden had the trust of Camellia teachers. Also at that time, these new grade-level teams began meeting monthly to examine benchmark or curriculum-embedded assessments. Teachers use the Sacramento City Reading First Open Court assessments to monitor student achievement during the school year. These assessments are given at the end of instructional units throughout the year. For kindergarten and Grade 1, assessments monitor fluency, spelling, writing, and sight words. For Grades 2 through 6, assessments monitor, fluency, comprehension, language skills, spelling, writing, and vocabulary. Teachers also use the Saxon assessments for math and have established writing benchmarks as well.

At the beginning, Ogden assisted in helping teachers interpret benchmark assessments. Teachers now review these assessments monthly in grade levels on their own. According to Ogden, he does not need to monitor grade-level review of benchmark assessments since Camellia teachers are driven to get better results and are constantly evaluating their own performance in comparison with how students are achieving. Teachers submit their six-week assessments to a clerk in the school office who inputs the data into the computer, and they are reviewed by Ogden.

Grade-Level Planning and Pacing

After the initial shift of teachers into grade-level teams, Ogden began working with teachers to pace and plan the curriculum. "I remember sitting in a grade-level meeting together with four very good teachers and saying let's get out our plan books and plan a unit together. They looked at me like I was insane. I remember going through the unit and no one wrote anything down. I thought at the time, this is not going to be easy. Now they do that on their own." Getting everyone aligned with standards-based curriculum and then planning together was a significant shift in the Camellia culture. However, the management of student behavior continued to be uniformly enforced by the teachers. The shift to planning and pacing the curriculum was similar. Prior to the Open Court and Saxon adoption, teachers were not coordinating the curriculum.

Intervening With Students

When the benchmark assessments show that certain students have fallen behind, teachers intervene during the language arts block in Open Court's "workshop" to meet with students to address these deficits. However, Camellia teachers are not so focused on intervention as they are on good first teaching. Teachers assess students daily and are immediately aware when students are not getting the concepts. They watch carefully when students are completing their work, ensuring that students are not "practicing errors." There is always someone watching students, either an instructional assistant or teacher, to make sure students are practicing correctly. Instructional assistants are trained monthly to assist teachers in the classroom. Ogden's philosophy is to give teachers every resource they need for students to avoid pulling any student out of the classroom. Only students receiving speech services are pulled from the classroom. Otherwise, it is the teacher's responsibility to assist students with learning. There is no resource specialist pull-out program.

> Camellia teachers are not so focused on intervention as they are on good first teaching. Teachers assess students daily and are immediately aware when students are not getting the concepts.

During grade-level meetings, teachers review areas assessed through the benchmark tests. Questions such as, "What are we going to do if a child is falling behind in comprehension?" are frequently asked. Teachers constantly brainstorm strategies for intervening with each specific assessed area. These strategies are implemented during Open Court's "workshop" time within the school day. This workshop occurs two or three times weekly when the instructional assistant is present. Students are placed in small groups, where the teacher and the aide address student weaknesses. Over the years, teachers have developed strategies for every area assessed through the benchmark tests. All intervention occurs totally within the classroom during the day.

THE ROLE OF THE LEADERSHIP TEAM AND GOVERNANCE

The leadership team at Camellia is primarily a decision-making group that works with the principal to resolve school issues, input new ideas, and address concerns. Faculty meetings are not used for this purpose. Ogden's philosophy is that staff meetings are a time to come together to learn something. With twenty or more people at faculty meetings, it is difficult to come to consensus on decisions. "I want staff input, but not twenty staff input," said Ogden. Faculty meetings are not a forum for a teacher to air his or her concerns.

Each grade level was asked to select one person to represent them at monthly meetings and at a meeting prior to the beginning of the school year. Each member serves one full year and the meetings are held after school. In the beginning, minutes were taken and shared with staff. However since Ogden organized this team structure, a majority of Camellia teachers have already served on the leadership team—so there is a lot more trust among the teachers now.

Most important decisions are run through this group, but Ogden feels that some decisions are his to make. For example, he made a decision to move seven teachers in his third year as principal. With this type of decision, the leadership team provides important counsel to Ogden—especially whether he should explain his decision at a grade-level meeting. The principal regards the leadership team as an input group, a "nuts-and-bolts" group, and the group with which he has the "hard conversations." In such a context, there can be in-depth discussion on any issue. Some of the nuts-and-bolts issues that may be dealt with, for example, might be adjustments made with the Saxon math curriculum this past year. A concern can be presented and Ogden can address it quicker within the leadership team than at the faculty meeting.

During this meeting, the team also builds an agenda for the faculty meeting that is held at the beginning of the month. A leadership team member facilitates the faculty meeting each month. Faculty meetings are also never a forum for staff to vote on issues. Carefully crafted plans are built through consensus. Consensus is built through the leadership team, within which plans are ironed out, problems solved, and then carried to the grade levels. Ogden is committed to keeping the focus on issues that pull the staff together rather than those that divide staff.

> Faculty meetings are also never a forum for staff to vote on issues. Carefully crafted plans are built through consensus.

There are some challenges with a leadership team structure, according to Ogden. With respect to the big decisions that have been made by Ogden, some of the teachers have not always agreed with him. "I say to the staff, this is a decision I need to make and I know the leadership team would have gone along with it." Having the same person representing a grade level could be a potential second problem. Ogden is convinced that, to have continuity, the same person must represent the grade level at each meeting for one year. When different people represent the grade level, there is a loss of continuity and communication.

Overall, Ogden embraces a philosophy of supporting teachers to do the critical job of teaching. "He handles situations clearly and decisively to free teachers for teaching," said the office manager. He provides anything that is needed for the teachers to do their job. He handles parents and issues that teachers feel are distractions to their teaching. This philosophy is consistent with the tradition established by Camellia's teachers over thirty years.

CAMELLIA'S NONNEGOTIABLE CORE VALUES AND SUSTAINING ELEMENTS

After several interviews with current and previous staff members, a distinct set of core values woven into the fabric of Camellia's culture became apparent.

1. **Student behavior is job number one.** "Teaching the kids what the rules are and how to act in the school is the most important thing we do," stated the teachers and the principal. *"We don't make the assumption that students know how to behave here. The first time a student is late for*

> "We don't make the assumption that students know how to behave here. The first time a student is late for school, we do something about it. The first time he or she misbehaves, we do something about it."

school, we do something about it. The first time he or she misbehaves, we do something about it." The teachers and the principal are completely committed to changing student behavior so that everyone knows how to act and to be successful at Camellia.

2. **The teachers are unified and take ownership for student behavior and learning.** It is expected that all Camellia teachers will take responsibility for their work with students and for the school. This is a core belief that is enforced by all teachers. It is a given that all teachers will work together—it is a team effort. There is extensive mentoring by senior staff regarding Camellia's history, core beliefs, and the proper role of what it

> The focus is not on the principal or the district, but on what they can do together to help students to be successful.

means to be a teacher at Camellia school. *The focus is not on the principal or the district, but on what they can do together to help students to be successful.* As a result of Camellia's strong unity, staff turnover is virtually nonexistent.

3. **Good first teaching is goal number one.** The strategic emphasis is on good first teaching to all students. The instructional level is diagnosed and addressed with the ultimate goal of taking these students to higher and higher levels of achievement. Teachers strongly believe in teaching 100 percent of the time directly and explicitly. When there are learning challenges, the teacher is

> There are no excuses or whining about the challenges encountered in the classroom. All teachers take responsibility for student learning.

asked, "What did you teach the first time?" *There are no excuses or whining about the challenges encountered in the classroom. All teachers take responsibility for student learning.*

4. **There is a consistent focus on higher and higher expectations for students.** As one teacher stated, "Our success with students has

given us confidence in our teaching practice and promotes the attitude of let's do a little more." Teacher ownership of this core value and collaboration with grade levels provide a system of checks and balances that ensures uniform implementation. Teachers are also continually reinforced in their teaching effectiveness when students are successful. Mary Marshall stated quite insightfully, *"When a teacher is successful in helping students to learn, it doesn't seem like work."*

> "When a teacher is successful in helping students to learn, it doesn't seem like work."

5. **Universal implementation is the key to consistency.** The reason Camellia has been so successful is that everyone implements the program or plan in the same manner. *Teachers know that they are not just responsible for their own classroom, but for all the students at Camellia.* They address the needs of students quickly and decisively. They plan together and implement their plans uniformly and then evaluate their progress. They assess their teaching daily with respect to student achievement. They are always making adjustments based on how students are learning.

> Teachers know that they are not just responsible for their own classroom, but for all the students at Camellia.

Camellia Elementary School has been a model of sustaining student achievement for more than thirty years. This school is a testimony to the lives of a core group of teachers who took the reins of an out-of-control school and implemented a behavior plan that transformed the school. They have committed themselves to making students successful academically and behaviorally, regardless of any counterproductive principal or district mandate. Even with an API of 896, these teachers are still trying to improve student achievement and student behavior. They have used student assessment data for years to provide insight on their instructional practice. They have achieved what some people would term the "impossible." In the words of Camellia's most veteran teacher, "It can be done and there are no ifs, ands, or buts about it."

LESSONS LEARNED FROM CAMELLIA ELEMENTARY SCHOOL

Student Discipline Has the Highest Priority. The ultimate goal is responsible and high-achieving students. This behavior is evident in passing periods, recess, and lunch. Hallways, the cafeteria, and recess areas are meticulously clean, exemplifying the priority and goal.

Classroom meetings held weekly to work out difficulties are largely led by students with oversight from teachers. The success teachers achieved with order and discipline led them to believe they could solve the learning issues within the school, which has propelled students to even higher levels of achievement.

Good First Teaching With Expected Universal Implementation by ALL Teachers. This mind-set developed from a core of teachers in the 1970s when there was "revolving-door leadership" from principals and the district. This band of teachers assumed responsibility for learning regardless of the current principal or district official.

A Core Belief That Teachers Working Together Will Make Great Things Happen for Students. Senior teachers mentor newer teachers in "the way it is done at Camellia." Teachers developed a culture of longevity—that is, if you come to teach at Camellia, you are expected to become an expert teacher and live out your teaching career there.

A Commitment to Universal Implementation of All Initiatives and an Unwavering Belief That All Students Can Achieve at High Levels. As the practices of order and discipline are embraced by all teachers, so other effective practices are embraced. This led Camellia from the bottom of all schools in the state to the very highest and to sustaining high achievement levels.

"You tell [teachers and administrators] that all kids can achieve and there are no ifs, ands, or buts about it."

4

Jefferson Elementary School, Carlsbad, California

A Culture of Collaboration

At first glance, Jefferson Elementary School doesn't appear to be a typical Title 1 school. The school is very attractive, clean, freshly painted, and remodeled, with modern playground equipment. Its location, right off the freeway, gives the initial impression of a "private school" with a majority of the parents residing in Carlsbad and commuting to San Diego. However, Jefferson School is a Title 1 school with 70 percent Latino, 24 percent white, and about 3 percent other ethnicities. Within this population of students, 44 percent are English-language learners and 64 percent are socioeconomically disadvantaged (SED) learners. Though faced with these challenges, Jefferson students have consistently improved in achievement year after year. This sustained achievement pattern could easily equal student achievement in a prestigious private school.

Jefferson can best be described as a community school where everyone wants to be there and relationships are highly valued. An environment where everyone is appreciated as an important piece of each student's success is a healthy characteristic of an achieving school culture. Few teachers or principals want to work in a caustic, grouchy school setting. Low-achieving schools often foster this kind of culture. However, at Jefferson and other sustaining schools, the atmosphere is charged with positive energy. It is clear that the importance of every staff member's contribution is valued at Jefferson.

> An environment where everyone is appreciated as an important piece of each student's success is a healthy characteristic of an achieving school culture.

As I sat in the office waiting to meet the principal, I could not help but notice the upbeat energy expressed by teachers and staff. Even with an onslaught of parents at the beginning of the school day, office staff warmly greeted each one, providing assistance in Spanish and English. "Everyone loves working here at Jefferson," a majority of staff commented to me throughout the day. Even the students rarely want to leave at the end of the school day. Many staff indicated that they have formed lasting friendships through their associations at Jefferson. Several teachers regularly meet to surf at the beach not far from the school. "We have so many amazing teachers here. We look out for each other, have fun together, and get involved in areas we are interested in," commented one teacher. This school additionally has strong community ties through service learning projects, and Communities Alive in Nature associations with local biologists and other community agencies. A purposeful connectedness is integrated in the fabric of this school's culture.

With a primary emphasis on building relationships provided by the leadership of an extremely gifted collaborative principal, Dr. Carol VanVooren, Jefferson has sustained student achievement for more than five years from an API of 574 to now 783. The Latino subgroup, the largest subgroup at Jefferson, has improved in student achievement from 492 to 749, a growth of 257 in schoolwide API. The SED learners who make up the second largest subgroup have improved even more dramatically than the Latino subgroup, showing growth of 251 over seven years. Jefferson teachers have clearly closed the gap between these two subgroups and the English-only subgroup.

Teachers take tremendous pride in this accomplishment. "It became a mission for us to achieve and to prove them wrong. We are going to show everyone." Where the gap in 1999 was 275 between the SEDs and English-only students, the gap has narrowed to 147. The Jefferson staff has managed to halt the widening gap between the SED/Latino subgroups and English-only subgroup, a pattern so prevalent in California. What's more, the overall achievement of all students has improved. This inspiring record of growth is shown in Table 4.1.

Jefferson is a Title 1 achieving school that has unquestionably broken the mold of what might typically be expected from schools facing similar challenges. In 1999, Jefferson School was named an Immediate

Table 4.1   API Scores for Jefferson Elementary School

Year	1999	2000	2001	2002	2003	2004	2005	Seven-Year Growth
Schoolwide API	574	631	680	697	732	750	783	209
Latino Subgroup API	492	559	627	652	691	711	749	257
White Subgroup API	760	815	815	819	853	855	883	123
SED API	485	564	623	642	689	714	736	251

Intervention of Underperforming Schools Program (IIUSP) school. This label created an immediate sense of urgency and a wake-up call to teachers and the recently hired principal. "We knew we had to do something or we would be in bigger trouble. Teachers knew they were going to have to change." After one month as principal, Dr. VanVooren put the challenge to her teachers at a staff meeting. "I stood in front of them and told teachers that we had a choice. Do we want to accept the IIUSP funding to improve student achievement? If we don't improve, I'm going to lose my job. But I am willing to take that risk if you are willing to do your part." VanVooren is convinced that at that time the teachers made an initial commitment to improve student achievement right then and there—that the culture of Jefferson changed from that day forward. VanVooren in her prior role as Jefferson's program coordinator had cultivated a significant number of collaborative relationships with these teachers. She assisted in the hiring of some of these teachers and worked hand-in-hand with them in the classroom. She is also convinced that, as Jefferson's new principal, past practice and traditions did not loom as large given the designation as an underperforming school with the accompanying mandates for change.

DEVELOPING A CULTURE OF COLLABORATION

Great successes of any kind in the school arena are always brought about through a collaborative team effort. Any principal must realize that it is not about what he or she can direct through individual efforts and mandates; it is always about relating, empowering, and motivating

> Any principal must realize that it is not about what he or she can direct through individual efforts and mandates; it is always about relating, empowering, and motivating the teachers who directly instruct the students.

the teachers who directly instruct the students. The challenge is to orchestrate staff in the school setting toward the common and preeminent goal—student learning. Principals must make every effort to build supportive relationships with teachers and staff, unleashing their talents and strengths toward student achievement goals. Through a primary focus on collaboration that valued each teacher's contribution, empowering him or her to be excellent instructors, Jefferson teachers dramatically improved student achievement over six years.

The Jefferson story began with a principal who is a master of collaboration on that September "day of commitment" to improve student achievement in 1999. Teachers knew VanVooren would do whatever it took to turn the school around and a majority of them joined her immediately. At the beginning of the 1999 school year, VanVooren uniquely was the principal of two schools—a K–4 school at the present site and a 5–6 school a mile away. By December 1999, the two schools combined to form one school at the present Jefferson site. Wisely, the principal and teachers had already made plans with IIUSP funding for collaboration time and social activities, since essentially both staffs did not even know each other. VanVooren commented that she had 100 staff when the two schools joined. "I arranged activities, ice breakers, and fun events so people would get to know each other. We played bingo with staff pictures to match the faces. There had also been few social events and so immediately I opened my home."

These events bonded the Jefferson staff together, according to teachers. These social events have led to very little attrition of the teaching staff, whereas prior to VanVooren becoming principal, they could not keep teachers at the school. This priority of collaborative relationships set the tone for teachers to be empowered and leadership to emerge from the staff.

The Upside of Differences

Putting the right staff in place at a school does not necessarily mean attracting personalities that are like-minded or even with the same temperament. Many times, differences in personality, skills, and ability are an asset in building collaboration. VanVooren's philosophy in working with people was shaped by her father, a college dean. She observed that her dad, a very athletic and disciplined man, frequently worked with an overweight staff member who smoked incessantly—someone who was entirely different from her physically fit dad. When asked why he would choose to work with him, her dad responded, "Between the two of us, we reach everyone at the school." She now looks for people who can offer skills and abilities that she can't offer. For example, she was able to hire a Latino male assistant principal and purposefully chose him "because he reaches people I can't reach and people who look at me in a different way."

A classified staff member who recently became a classroom teacher at

> Putting the right staff in place at a school does not necessarily mean attracting personalities that are like-minded or even with the same temperament. Many times differences in personality, skills, and ability are an asset in building collaboration.

Jefferson is another example. This teacher still has close friendships with other classified staff now that she is part of the regular teaching staff. However, the principal knows that if this teacher is participating in a school activity, the other classified staff will participate as well. This young teacher is able to bridge the gap between both classified and certificated staff members. "People who have different skills than I have are the kind of people I really want to empower," VanVooren stated.

Another example of differences in skills and personalities contributing to the collaborative process is Jefferson's literacy resource teacher, who is "black and white" about collecting interim assessment data. She is rigorous about teachers turning in their data correctly on time on a certain date. "We have different leadership styles and people respond to her. If it were done my way, the data wouldn't get collected." Having a difference in personalities helps balance the entire staff. VanVooren feels that listening to her adversaries is a definite asset in building a collaborative culture. "They are the ones I need to check with the most because they aren't thinking the same way I am and it is good to get that information." Capitalizing on personality differences as well as promoting the skills and talents of others is an important piece of building a collaborative culture.

Learning to value each individual in the school organization, no matter how variant the personalities, is critical to a principal's success in raising student achievement. Many times as a principal myself I have had to "bite my tongue" in the early days of establishing an achieving culture when negativity ruled. It took deliberate effort every day to reshape the negative comments and attitudes into positive results. Appreciating everyone (though difficult) as a valuable asset to student success was key in creating a high-achieving culture.

Replacing Staff

When Jefferson became an IIUSP school, some teachers elected to leave. The principal remembered one teacher standing over her stating, "Do you want me to stay here?" With her heart fluttering, she recalled that she did not have a comfortable relationship with that teacher and really didn't believe it would benefit the staff for that teacher to stay. She responded that she would love to have her stay but wanted her to do what she felt comfortable with. The teacher said, "Well I'm leaving." VanVooren remembers wishing her well and being sure it was right for Jefferson and right for that teacher to leave.

Every wise principal knows that it is vital to hire teachers who not only have excellent teaching skills but, just as important, also have those interpersonal skills to assimilate well with the rest of the instructional team.

> Every wise principal knows that it is vital to hire teachers who not only have excellent teaching skills but, just as important, also have those interpersonal skills to assimilate well with the rest of the instructional team.

VanVooren has had the opportunity to hire key teachers and staff for Jefferson. In her role as special projects coordinator for Jefferson prior to becoming principal, she spent three years assisting the previous principal in hiring the "right staff" to support a bilingual program. Teachers at Jefferson were very familiar with her because she had helped to hire many of them and had worked with them. Having already established positive working relationships with the Jefferson staff was an advantage in transitioning Jefferson from a low-achieving to a high-achieving culture.

Then too, VanVooren's role as student teacher supervisor at California State University, San Marcos, allowed her to introduce new teachers to the staff and watch them in action at Jefferson. She doesn't hire new teachers unless she has had an opportunity to supervise them directly. Through experience as a high-school teacher, assistant principal, and Title VII coordinator, she appreciates the benefits of male teachers at a site. Over the years, eight men have joined the elementary teaching ranks, helping to bring balance and different expertise to the staff, as well as provide important role models for students.

Every principal should have a direct role in selecting and cultivating teachers who will work well together to create a high-achieving culture and to support the instructional mission of improving student achievement. I have found that discovering teachers who were passionate about helping students achieve was more important at times than their teaching credentials. Additionally, finding teachers who will fit with the school's culture is also important. Getting the right people in position is critical not only to sustaining a high-achieving culture but also to the ongoing quest to be a great school.

Reluctant Staff

At Jefferson, some staff members are slow to change or improve their practice. Even with a hand-picked staff, there will always be those who struggle. Teachers at Jefferson know who these teachers are. Because they expect Jefferson to be a great school, they assume a nurturing role for reluctant staff and new teachers. Grade-level leaders and all teachers belonging to that grade level have made it a core value that they must collectively work together. "The grade-level leader fosters the planning with other members of the grade level. We feel that everyone has to participate." Reluctant teachers, as well as new teachers, are not given the option to isolate themselves because they are moved along by peer pressure and the collaborative core values of the group. "We take responsibility for the grade level because our scores are being reported," stated one grade-level leader.

Key teachers regularly take care of these reluctant staff members, including them in the upcoming training, providing copies of lesson plan materials, or calling them at home on weekends to offer encouragement. VanVooren credits this response to the supportive family culture of many Hispanic members on her staff. "My teachers have brought them around in a positive way without my having to be a heavy hand on them." Teachers will also come to VanVooren to share worries they have about other teachers. Instead of the principal going directly back to confront the teacher having trouble, VanVooren brainstorms with the concerned teacher as to what can be done to help the struggling teacher. Less effective principals might panic and begin to devise a strategy to dismiss the teacher. Instead, solutions are discussed to help the struggling teacher. "I could talk to her but what do *you* think we should do?" VanVooren will say to help teachers learn to work out their differences and misunderstandings.

> Reluctant teachers, as well as new teachers, are not given the option to isolate themselves because they are moved along by peer pressure and the collaborative core values of the group.

In many schools, it might be seen as a betrayal that teachers would talk about other teachers to the principal. When asked about this, one grade-level leader commented, "Carol is good at keeping confidences and helping to guide teachers along." Because such a high level of trust and confidence has been established with the staff by VanVooren, the real instructional issues or other issues can be quickly addressed. When there is a lack of trust, infighting, or politics at a school, improvement efforts are delayed or even crippled. Building trust and confidence in teachers is job number one for any new principal. Without an atmosphere of trust, any worthwhile efforts at improving student achievement will become hung up in issues that relate to a prior regime and the hurts from the past. With reluctant teachers, VanVooren has the wisdom to trust the leadership team to act first to help develop teacher expertise while she remains on the sidelines to assist with ongoing problem solving.

> Building trust and confidence in teachers is job number one for any new principal. Without an atmosphere of trust, any worthwhile efforts at improving student achievement will become hung up in issues that relate to a prior regime and the hurts from the past.

Emerging Leadership

It is imperative that a principal encourage and facilitate shared leadership among teachers and staff. In effective schools, every member of the school community has the responsibility and the authority to take appropriate leadership roles. At Jefferson, staff leadership began to evolve from early collaborative relationships cultivated by the principal. At first, teachers were hesitant to take on leadership roles. Teachers would comment, "Isn't that the principal's job?" or "Aren't you supposed to tell us what to do?"

In response, training and support were delivered to teachers, with books on current educational research and workshops such as Marzano's (2003) *What Works in Schools*, which deals with mentoring. Just recently, the leadership team made recommendations for revising Jefferson's school homework policy using *Classrooms That Work* by Cunningham and Allington (2006). VanVooren, from the beginning, made it very clear to teachers they are needed and valued; she encouraged them to take on leadership roles such as grade-level leaders, P.E. specialists, literacy specialists, and others. Amazingly, these specialized roles emerged naturally from the group without negative competition or rancor. Teachers participated in what they termed as logical staff choices for leadership roles in consultation with VanVooren.

A consistent emphasis on an "even playing field," no teacher "favorites," and treating everyone the same was pursued by VanVooren. "I believe in them and I need their help. Collectively, we have a broader perspective with all of us rather than just my perspective," stated the principal. Sometimes the choice for grade-level leadership might not be the choice made by the principal but would be someone the teachers felt supported them and someone who would get the job done. It is important though to understand that Jefferson's principal is involved in expressing her own opinion regarding these decisions. The difference is that she values the input of her staff and does not execute the power of her position to force a choice, preferring to collaborate to reach a consensus decision.

"At Jefferson, there is not one leader but many leaders, from both certificated and classified staff," commented one grade-level leader. All staff are expected to take on responsibilities and real jobs at Jefferson. For the Jefferson staff members, understanding their value and importance as a leader has multiplied their effort and effectiveness in helping students. This point of view is a credit to VanVooren for effectively distributing leadership across the school. These jobs govern all aspects of the school—committee chairmanships, grade-level responsibilities, computer technology, community events, and even Saturday intervention activities. When a teacher becomes part of Jefferson, it is clear that

> When a teacher becomes part of Jefferson, it is clear that person is expected to become a part of the culture; that is, to contribute much the same as a family member would.

person is expected to become a part of the culture; that is, to contribute much the same as a family member would.

Even in the hiring process, where both teachers and other staff members participate with the principal, candidates are evaluated according to their strengths and contributions that they can make to Jefferson. Candidates coming in must "fit the culture" and immediately become an active contributor. "When we interview teachers, we are looking for strengths that they will contribute at Jefferson." As a result, Jefferson has had the same core staff for more than six years. No one wants to leave. With recent declining enrollment and the elimination of classes this past year, a heart-wrenching experience occurred when two teachers had to leave the school. Since no one wanted to leave, the district office finally made the choice. Often during my visit, teachers commented how painful it was to lose these teachers. Jefferson also had to reduce certificated full-time tutors to hourly employees because of budget constraints. All of these tutors came back to Jefferson to work in intervention programs despite a severe pay cut and loss of benefits. When teachers are valued, respected, and feel they are achieving a great mission for students, it is worth far more than money.

Decision-Making Processes

Grade-level leadership has become a very significant factor in improving Jefferson's student achievement. The distribution of power to these grade-level leaders by the principal served to establish the necessary infrastructure for multiplying effort and coordinating all aspects of the IIUSP plan. Plus, the power distribution awakened in staff the desire to assume accountability for the improvement process. Grade-level leaders in turn provided support for resolving the inevitable uncertainties and hesitancies that accompany the changes demanded by the plan.

Every school leadership team that is "under the gun" to improve begins with uncertainty and fear. One grade-level leader commented that it took one year for the leadership team to fully accept their role as a leader. What assisted their acceptance and enabled them to function well was the book *How to Make Meetings Work* by Michael Doyle (1976). VanVooren led discussions on this book as members of the leadership team were learning to assume their "facilitator" role. Throughout the year, the principal steadfastly encouraged them and consistently believed in them as they worked through their own uncertainties.

Right from the beginning, leaders were selected and chosen by the grade level. Typically they have greater peer acceptance, especially when the principal is working with these leaders to initiate change in the school culture. Among all high-achieving schools I have visited, leaders are selected in this manner. These leaders serve for one or more years. The length of time a leader remains in this position varies according to the grade level. These leaders meet formally each month and adhere to an organized agenda. Items are not discussed that are not on the agenda. Any teacher can submit items or concerns for the agenda via a grade-level leader or the principal. An established agenda and minutes of these meetings create transparency, thus maintaining trust with teachers that is essential to the improvement process.

Recommendations from the leadership team are taken to staff meetings, which are held twice each month. Grade-level leaders take turns in leading faculty meetings, recording the minutes, and so on. VanVooren again insists teachers take ownership for the decisions made during these meetings. One faculty meeting each month is devoted to schoolwide issues, and one meeting a month is devoted to reviewing student achievement data relating to curriculum and instruction issues. Minutes are taken at these meetings and a designated "food" person makes sure there are always refreshments. Recommendations and proposed plans made between the leadership team and faculty meetings are taken to Jefferson's School Site Council for schoolwide decision making and funding.

Jefferson's leadership model is a sustaining process that would continue to be in place should VanVooren leave the school. As a true leader, she has successfully guided teachers in taking responsibility for their school. Teachers are assuming leadership roles, participating in decisions, and assuming responsibility for those decisions. Most schools where leadership is shared are successful, sustaining, and continuing to improve.

Grade-level leaders facilitate curricular planning with teachers at each grade level. Grade levels usually plan together once each week. It is expected that all teachers will attend at an agreed-on time for planning. It is not an option for teachers to miss this planning time. Planning is essential to implementing the proper pacing of standards instruction through curricular material. It is also a time when grade-level events are planned and coordinated, such as fieldtrips, special programs, and the like. All teachers share in the responsibilities and execution of grade-level instruction. "There is an expectation that each teacher will be taking responsibility for some leadership role in the grade level," commented one grade-level leader. "Everyone has a job to do."

Advice to Principals

The number one element in establishing a collaborative culture is *trust*. The principal is key to creating an environment in which there is trust, or the lack of it. Trust is established when principals are true to their word—they say what they mean and mean what they say. Teachers will trust when there are no "politics between the lines" or hidden agendas in what the principal might say. VanVooren recalled working in a school where everyone was "hiding their cards," afraid to be honest. "Why would you reveal your honest thoughts and ideas to have the principal embarrass you or tell you that you didn't do a good job?" This happened with a teacher who implemented a new idea with the curriculum prior to VanVooren becoming principal. She was ordered by the principal to stop the innovation. That principal took away what the teacher was excited about and destroyed trust. When politics are present, staff members will not communicate their true feelings or ideas or even make suggestions to problem solve issues within the school. They will only say what is "safe" for fear of reprisal. Where politics are absent, everyone on the staff is free to be honest and willing to take risks, to bring forth ideas to solve problems, to try new instructional strategies, or to take on a new leadership role.

> When politics are present, staff members will not communicate their true feelings or ideas or even make suggestions to problem solve issues within the school. They will only say what is "safe" for fear of reprisal.

There is a difference between the trust of a friend and the ethical trust of leadership. With any principal, the ethical decision must be first and foremost. Sometimes the decision is not what teachers would like for their needs, but it is the right decision for the school. The principal must "put the elephant on the table" even if it is bad news. VanVooren commented on a recent situation where one of the teachers sadly had cancer and the other teachers wanted to give their sub days to allow that teacher time away. This offer was not unusual since relationships are highly valued among the Jefferson staff. After checking with the district office, VanVooren found out that this could not be done. She had to deliver the bad news that the problem could not be solved in the way the teachers wanted. Jefferson teachers were disappointed with the district's answer. Instead they raised funds to help the teacher. Another example of the right decision can be found in the manner in which the principal deals with teacher absence from faculty meetings. VanVooren insists that they meet with her to "make up" the meeting. Because faculty meetings are a highly collaborative process where joint decisions are made, it is critical to get teachers on the same page. VanVooren makes a deliberate effort to meet with teachers to establish that point. "Sometimes you have to hold to what is true and ethical. People respect someone who can lead like that. If principals handle the tough decisions, teachers know that you won't make exceptions and they will trust that you will do the right things for them and the school." When principals develop a school context where trust and honesty are practiced and valued, a collaborative culture emerges.

JEFFERSON'S NONNEGOTIABLE CORE VALUES

At the center of Jefferson's core values is the collaboration of *all* staff. This collaborative or collegial working of teachers refers to professional interaction that includes precise and concrete talk about instruction, cooperative planning and design of teaching materials, and the sharing of technical knowledge in an instructional context with other teachers. Working collaboratively has strengthened teacher confidence and competence, which in turn has improved student achievement as documented in the API for Jefferson. When teachers are isolated, many times resistance and negativity are caused by a lack of confidence about the effectiveness of their teaching and fear of change. Collaboration with grade-level colleagues reduces fear and elevates confidence. Another byproduct of collaboration is the elevated expectation for student performance, because Jefferson teachers now believe that they can positively affect student achievement and their students can continuously perform at a high level.

When VanVooren became Jefferson's principal, she cemented the mission of improving Jefferson's achievement through collaborative relationships. Collaboration was one of her core values from the beginning. The expectation was set from the beginning that all staff would collaborate. "No one can close their door and do their own thing. When we have meetings, they must be there. There are no exceptions," stated VanVooren. She definitely feels that when teachers are not at critical meetings, they don't all hear the same information, the upshot of which is a lack of coordinated implementation on consensus decisions directly affecting student achievement. This translates to, "I don't have to do what the rest of the staff is doing." The principal believes that there is a need to continuously build a bond between teachers to share what they are doing with students and to be talking about effective practices and/or challenges in the classroom and working effectively with parents. Teachers have commented to VanVooren that "they are nervous of what they miss" if they are absent from a meeting.

All teachers must participate in training to improve instructional practice. Sometimes the training is on Saturdays due to a lack of other time options. Teachers have commented that VanVooren motivates teachers to come even on Saturdays. As one teacher put it, "She has a winsome way of making us feel that if we aren't at the training, we will miss something, and we don't want to miss anything." VanVooren firmly believes that teachers must be there to foster collaborative talking that will lead teachers to adopt new instructional practices. When teachers are not there, they are left behind and may become estranged from other members of their grade level. Training coupled with collaboration helps a staff integrate new instructional practices within teaching. Collaborative talking also assists teachers in developing plans for implementation within the classroom. The Jefferson staff has participated in a variety of training workshops provided through Dataworks, Marzano (McRel), ETS Pulliam, Pam Noli, and so on that have made a difference in their instructional practices.

USING BENCHMARK DATA TO TARGET INSTRUCTION

According to Jefferson teachers and the principal, the goals in the school plan are simple: (1) advance each student's achievement at least one year and (2) develop well-rounded students through enrichment activities. Jefferson has band, percussion, and choir programs, as well as art and P.E. instruction, which are rarely seen these days at elementary schools in California. Both the principal and the teachers I talked with did not have to drag out and dust off the school plan to talk knowingly about what they were doing. It was obvious to me that when teachers know what they are doing and why they are doing it, it is emblazoned on their souls. There is no wasted energy in inventing a purpose or developing excuses for not improving student achievement.

The school is sharply focused on the business of improving student achievement through the use of student data, which proved to be invaluable because the teachers came to actually believe that turning the school around was possible. One teacher commented, "Every year we have struggles and we ask the question, are we making a difference? Then we see the scores going up and we know we are making a difference." They had begun using a series of benchmark tests four times during the year to monitor student learning in English language arts beginning in kindergarten and extending through second grade. These tests were based on achievement of reading skills identified by the standards. Benchmark tests allowed teachers to see individual student results immediately. In the beginning, teachers felt that this assessment took them away from instruction. Now these assessments are an ingrained pattern of delivering instruction. "Each time they assess students, they feel so empowered about the effect they are having on students that it confirms for them that they are on the right path," stated VanVooren.

There is great power in using regular assessments to provide feedback on instruction. Benchmarks that reveal what reading skills are in place and which are not empower teachers to address specific skills that are weak or are missing. Prior to Jefferson's defined process of examining data, teachers could only gain information from assessment processes in their individual classrooms and "hope" that students would do well on the state test. Common benchmark assessments given throughout the year aligned to the standards allow the teacher to measure student performance more strategically and to determine what standards have been mastered and what standards have yet to be mastered. Establishing a grade-level data process eliminates the guesswork and allows teachers to see how students are performing across a grade level. Collaborative discussion focuses on strategies that are working with students so that a strategic plan is developed.

Data were first systematically collected in kindergarten through second grade with the help of a very skilled first-grade teacher, Jo Fitzpatrick, who came to Jefferson. She is a very organized and skilled teacher who is highly respected. She has thirty-five years of experience in literacy-based reforms, particularly in the primary grades, and has authored several books on early literacy. She brought much expertise to teaching low-achieving students and was later welcomed by the staff as Jefferson's literacy resource teacher.

She was particularly helpful in working with teachers in aligning curriculum to the English language arts standards. In 1999, Jefferson did not have access to the state-adopted standards-based curriculum, which was the case for many schools in California. Fitzpatrick also assisted in developing an early literacy program that consisted of the following.

- Extensive professional development for all teachers, especially those teaching in the primary grades, led by teachers who were taking on a leadership role, such as grade-level leaders.
- Regular detailed assessment of all students as they progressed through a sequence of standards from initial phonemic awareness to reading with comprehension.
- Implementation of small-group instruction and ability grouping of students to address specific needs. At specific times during language arts, students are grouped homogeneously to meet their specific reading needs. This is not to be confused with tracking, which involves homogeneously grouping for the entire day.
- Targeted intervention within the classroom, after school, or on Saturdays for struggling students based on assessment profiles.

To monitor the progress of all students, the principal meets quarterly with each teacher to review student assessment data and to develop a plan for intervention. Initially, every teacher works with the literacy resource teacher to complete a series of quarterly assessments that are reported to the principal. Teachers are responsible for preparing a class color-coded profile of each student's assessment data. Together, VanVooren and each teacher discuss each student and record his or her progress. VanVooren takes notes and questions each teacher regarding students who are struggling and what is being done to intervene. Teachers are encouraged to partner with the literacy resource teacher for assistance. Figure 4.1 presents an example of a Quarterly Class Profile, and Figure 4.2, an Assessment Recording Form, both used to monitor student performance.

VanVooren meets with each teacher four times during the year, conducting more than 120 teacher conferences to review this data with teachers. The data collected across all grade levels are posted on a long "data wall" just outside the teacher workroom to remind teachers of current schoolwide student achievement data and to motivate them to continue to persevere to achieve the next set of instructional goals with students.

Teachers also participate in *monthly* "data meetings" (Schmoker, 2006) with their grade levels or a combination of grade levels. Substitute teachers are provided through Title 1 funds so teachers can meet during a morning to analyze student achievement data. Allowing this much time for grade-level meetings during the school day is unusual. Teachers are not often allowed the luxury of time during the day to look at assessment data. There is an unspoken expectation that teachers will examine such data on their own.

Figure 4.1   Quarterly Class Profile Example

Teacher _Sample_				Grade _1st_
Quarterly Class Profile				
Skill Area _Phonemic Awareness_				

Levels	Testing Quarters			
	1st.	2nd.	3rd.	4th.
	10/0	2/0	3/0 5/0	
Level R	‖ 2	0		0
Level 1	‖‖ ⫽ 7	0		0
Level 2	卌 卌 I 11	0		0
Level 3	0	11	1	0
Level 4	0	卌 卌 18 卌 卌	卌 ‖‖ 19 卌 卌	‖ 2
Level 5	0	0		卌 ‖‖ 18 卌 卌
	20	20	20	20

Instructional Implications

Level	Target Areas
Purple group	Consonant digraphs and blends for students at Level 3
Blue group	Reading and writing comprehension for the entire class
Green group	

Figure 4.2 Assessment Recording Form Example

Name <u>Sample</u>   School _____

Grade _____   Teacher _____

Individual Student End of Year Composite

Please enter date of mastery in each appropriate category.

Kindergarten. . . green   First. . . yellow   Second. . . orange

Level 5	12/02 Manipulat.	Vowel Comb. Multisyllab.	6/03 Vowel Combination	<u>Accuracy</u> ___ <u>Comp.</u> ___	6/03 Self-Monitoring	10/02 5 Point Story	Resolution Writing
Level 4	9/02 6/02 Segment.	6/03 Long Vowels Spellings	3/03 Blend Clusters	<u>Accuracy 94</u> 6/03 <u>Comp. 80</u> 3/03	12/02 Story Context	6/02 Story Walk	Sequential Event (Elaboration)
Level 3	12/01 Sound Isolation	6/02 Short Vowels	12/02 Long/Short Vowel Disc.	<u>Accuracy 96</u> 12/02 <u>Comp. 100</u>	6/02 Structural Clues	3/02 3 Point Story	5/03 Letter Writing
Level 2	12/01 Oral Blending	6/02 Sight Vocab.	6/02 Short 3/02 Vowels	<u>Accuracy 94</u> 9/02 <u>Comp. 80</u> 6/02	12/01 Phonetic Cueing	11/01 Sent. Exp	4/03 Narrative (Setting. Char. Plot)
Level 1	12/01 Rhyme	12/01 Consonant & Digraphs	12/01 Consonant 6/01 Digraphs	<u>Accuracy 96</u> 6/02 <u>Comp. 100</u>	3/01 Predictable Patterns	10/01 Pattern Sentences	2/03 Story Development (Beg/Mid/End)
Level R	3/01 Auditory Discrim.	9/00 Pre-Alphabetic	12/00 Consonant Matching	<u>Accuracy 100</u> 6/02 <u>Comp. 100</u>	9/00 Picture Clues	9/00 Concepts	12/02 Expository (Descriptive sequence)
	Phonemic Awareness	Alphabetic Principle	Decoding Skills	Oral Reading Comprehension	A.L. Strategies	Writing Stages	Process Writing

Analysis:
Please add end of the year comments, date, indicate grade level and sign.

When grade levels first began meeting, VanVooren attended each of these meetings to coach grade-level leaders and to help them follow a protocol for data analysis. She attended all of these meetings for two years and now attends these grade-level data meetings as the need arises. VanVooren is convinced that grade-level data meetings are a sustaining process at Jefferson. When grade levels have met, "They come back like they have seen a vision." When grade levels don't meet, the principal said that the grade level seems scattered and unconnected, and their coordinated instructional implementation suffers. Data meetings give teachers at a grade level an honest look at how students are performing and, based on that performance, develop a better plan than if they were isolated in a classroom. At grade-level data meetings, teachers discuss effective instructional strategies, assist newer teachers, and coordinate all of the work at the grade level.

Let there be no doubt that most teachers must be coached on how to analyze student data and then to use that data to alter curriculum and instruction. This analysis will not be done without concentrated focus and effort. Time must be given for this crucial step to occur. Making the assumption that teachers actually know how to look at data and alter their instruction is a mistake. Many administrators go through the motions of collecting data and then never show teachers how to use that data in the classroom. This is one of the main reasons why teachers are against benchmark assessments. Another reason assessments are unpalatable is that when assessments are collected, teachers rarely are given the results until months later when the data are no longer useful.

USING DATA TO INTERVENE WITH STUDENTS

Without the collection of student achievement data across the school year, there can be little intervention that will have any promise of success. Assessment data show where each student's deficiencies in learning exist. Current assessment data reveal student performance on the standards most recently taught in the classroom. Thus, if the teacher is able to analyze this data, he or she can help students attain mastery of specific standards more quickly, as well as intervene with those who did not master those standards. The secret to improving each student's achievement is addressing specific deficiencies quickly with strategic instruction in a variety of contexts, ideally within the classroom setting first.

> The secret to improving each student's achievement is addressing specific deficiencies quickly with strategic instruction in a variety of contexts, ideally within the classroom setting first.

At Jefferson, struggling students are identified through quarterly benchmark assessments that form the basis for initial placement of Jefferson students prior to each school year. The outgoing grade level completes a student placement card consisting of the benchmark assessments collected across the year, as well as other data such as behavior concerns, special needs, and language level. Both the outgoing and incoming grade level place students into classes. The principal and grade-level leaders monitor where low-achieving students are placed. Effort is made to create a balanced class with not too many groups of low-achieving students and always a middle or higher group of students within the classroom. Careful placement of students helps to avoid wide variances in ability levels, enabling the teacher to be more effective in meeting the needs of students. Positioning students in classrooms strategically based on their assessment is another smart strategy for success. Eliminating the wide variance in levels of students gives teachers greater opportunity to better meet the needs of students.

After the school year has started, end-of-the-year benchmark assessments and STAR data for each student provide a starting place for teachers. Intervention is planned first and foremost in a variety of groupings within the classroom for struggling students. All Jefferson teachers have been trained in effective reading instruction and are set up with flex tables (i.e., tables arranged for small groups of students for flexible grouping throughout the day).

Twelve certificated teachers serve as tutors, partnering with grade-level teachers to intervene with students. These tutors are funded through Title 1 funds. Tutors work within the classroom or pull students for more intensive intervention for brief periods during the school day, after school, or on Saturdays. These flexible groupings change frequently as students improve and exit the intervention group.

Jefferson tutors are very flexible in addressing different needs across different grade levels. For example, when there were several older, recently arrived Latino students, one of the tutors developed a newcomers' class so that they could learn beginning English-language skills immediately. The "story queen," a skilled language arts teacher, works with students on writing after school.

The principal is adamant that once a student's deficiency is remediated, he or she will exit the group so that a student will not become "stuck" in intervention forever. "The kids know that they will exit the intervention group once they have met certain standards. It is much more motivating to students to catch up when intervention is handled this way."

Certificated tutors were put in place by the district to deliver high-quality instruction for struggling students. Typically, districts or schools use classified instructional assistants. Now with the No Child Left Behind requirements for instructional delivery, every student in a Title 1 school must have instruction by those who are "highly qualified." Having certificated tutors from the beginning has provided consistent intervention for Jefferson students.

Another successful intervention is the extended learning class for students who are not ready for first grade. Most schools in California have a half-day kindergarten program. For a school with a large number of English learners, this is frequently not enough time for a majority of them to learn the language arts skills for success in first grade. The extended learning class is a two-year program for students who do not master initially the kindergarten standards and for those who are not developmentally ready. Parents must sign a retention form giving permission for their child to be in this class.

A highly skilled teacher instructs this class with an entirely different curriculum. It is not a repeat of the kindergarten curriculum but is based on a combination of kindergarten and first-grade standards. If a student suddenly catches on during the school year and the assessments show he or she is ready for first grade, the student "skips" up to a regular first-grade class. "As a result of this extended learning program over the years, very few students are ever recommended for retention," stated VanVooren.

Parents form an integral partnership with Jefferson's intervention and instructional program for students. More than 90 percent of Jefferson parents turn out for teacher conferences and other schoolwide events. Grade-level teachers have enlisted parent support of the instructional program through monthly parent nights, the Jefferson Parent Institute, ESL classes, and other special classes and events. Monthly grade-level parent nights consist of teachers presenting the focus for the grade-level curriculum as well as teaching parents how to help their children at home. Teachers feel that these sessions help parents understand how they can partner with the school in the education of their children. These meetings are well attended, particularly in the primary grades. Any materials that parents might need are prepared by the teachers and supplied to parents. For example, fifth-grade teachers spent time teaching parents how division is taught in the United States. The Parent Institute has helped more than 300 newcomer parents become oriented to Jefferson School and the community. Community agencies such as the Carlsbad Police Department also work with Jefferson parents in the Parent Project to help with parenting skills and child safety. Overall the Jefferson school community is united in helping students be successful. This integrated support system is directly attributable to and sustained by Jefferson's culture of collaboration.

JEFFERSON'S SUSTAINING ELEMENTS

The most vital sustaining elements and practices identified by Jefferson teachers and the principal are as follows.

- **Using assessments to monitor student learning.** The use of benchmark assessments to monitor student learning throughout the year has become a powerful tool to guide instruction. Analyzing and reflecting on individual student data have revealed strengths and weaknesses in their instruction, helped teachers align curriculum to the standards, and identified areas for improvement and further training.

- **Strategic intervention with students who are falling behind.** When students fall behind as shown by benchmark assessments, intervention first begins in the classroom. Teachers are expected to use flexible grouping, as well as teaming with the grade level to assist struggling students. Certificated tutors work with grade-level teachers to additionally work with students within the regular school day. After-school classes and Saturday school are provided to provide more intensive intervention with students. The effectiveness of intervention is monitored by teachers who know how to analyze assessments and then turn that data into instruction.

- **Emphasis on collaboration.** The collaboration of staff is another important variable in sustaining student achievement at Jefferson. All Jefferson staff members believe that they are there to make a difference in the lives of students. Teachers have confidence in themselves and their colleagues. They see themselves as making a unique contribution to Jefferson. They are always looking to improve their practice. They all share in the leadership and accountability of the school. They see themselves as a family working together.

- **A pattern of continuous improvement.** Everyone at Jefferson is proud of the school and the achievements of students. However, there is a steadfast determination to continually improve. With all of the high-performing schools in Carlsbad, the school continues to persevere, as it is still the lowest performing school in the district. However, Jefferson has closed the achievement gap significantly in the past two years. The Jefferson staff will continue to look for better ways to help students be even more successful. "It has become a mission for us to achieve—to prove to them that we are successful."

Finally, Jefferson has become a school that is constantly improving not only student achievement but also the lives of students. The staff is committed to the students and each other. They are not disheartened by the challenges of poverty and language that students face. They continue to excel chiefly due to the way they work with each other to improve their practice. Collaboration at Jefferson has resulted in more than five years of improved student achievement, a definite testimony to its success.

LESSONS LEARNED FROM JEFFERSON ELEMENTARY SCHOOL

Collaboration by and With All Staff to Improve Student Achievement. Teachers are empowered to become leaders, and relationships among all members of the school community are highly valued. A new teacher or staff member is expected to contribute to the school and become part of the school community.

No Option for a Teacher or Staff Member to "Opt Out" of School Responsibilities or Become Isolated. Each member is expected to uniquely give his or her best to the students, parents, and the staff. When teachers miss staff meetings, they make them up. When there is a major training of an instructional strategy, all teachers and staff are expected to be there. These norms are imposed by all of the members of the school community.

Differences Among Staff Are Strengths, Not Weaknesses. There is a sense of valuing what teachers and staff members can contribute to meet the overall goal of encouraging student achievement and servicing parents.

Teacher-Leaders Preserve a Solid Infrastructure of Accountability. When teachers experience difficulty, teacher-leaders make it their responsibility to intervene to support, teach, train, or just become a listening ear. The collaborative structure is so important that when the school needed to lose two teachers to declining enrollment, no one wanted to leave.

"An expectation for collaboration was set from the beginning. No one can close their door and do their own thing. When we have meetings, they must be there. There are no exceptions."

5

Rosita Elementary School, Garden Grove, California

A Culture of Clarity

Nestled within an urban, high-poverty setting, Rosita Elementary School is a safe haven for 706 immigrant students in kindergarten through sixth grade. Rosita is one of forty-seven elementary schools in the Garden Grove Unified School District, a 2004 national recipient of the prestigious Eli Broad Award. Arriving at Rosita, I was first impressed by the warm reception I received from the office staff. Impressive also was the genuine enthusiasm and high energy of the principal, Dr. Gabriela Mafi. Throughout my observation, I noticed a sense of intentionality and purposeful practice in the demeanor of Rosita teachers. It was also obvious from my conversations with teachers that this faculty cares very much about the children who attend Rosita. "Every teacher considers the children of Rosita as their own," several teachers shared. "We are a family together." Nearly 70 percent of Rosita students are immigrants or first-generation Americans from Mexico, while the remaining 30 percent are from Vietnam. "Except for four students, every student in our school is a child of color," Mafi is quick to say in describing the school's clientele.

Table 5.1   API Scores for Rosita Elementary School

Year	1999	2000	2001	2002	2003	2004	2005	Seven-Year Growth
Schoolwide API	572	638	659	681	739	779	792	220
Asian Subgroup API	705	768	770	785	829	873	887	182
Latino Subgroup API	510	577	607	641	701	736	749	239
SED API	564	616	644	672	741	773	784	220

Since a majority of students are immigrants or first-generation Americans, 67 percent of the students are English learners and 79 percent of the over-all student population is high poverty. It is no wonder that this staff feel successful and proud of the now more than five-year record of sustained student academic achievement.

For seven years, Rosita students have steadily and dramatically increased their academic performance, going beyond both their Academic Performance Index (API) and the No Child Left Behind federally required AYP targets, as demonstrated in Table 5.1. Rosita began the journey to high achieving in 1999 with an API of 572, which identified the school as an Immediate Intervention of Underperforming Schools Program (IIUSP) for California. In seven years, Rosita has grown to an API of 792, or an increase of 220. Remarkably, Rosita grew substantially in every subgroup population (Hispanic, Asian, and socioeconomically disadvantaged groups), satisfying the No Child Left Behind AYP measure. This growth is almost miraculous with 67 percent of the student population being comprised of English learners. This kind of improvement could only come from a total school commitment involving the leadership of two principals, teachers committed to expecting the best from students and themselves, and a district steadfastly supporting their efforts to do what was necessary.

BUILDING A HIGH-ACHIEVING CULTURE

How did the transformation to a high-performing, Title 1 school take place? The process began and has been sustained at Rosita Elementary School by the deliberate, precise, and joint actions of two very talented principals and a committed band of teachers. Principal Kathy Roe left the school in June of 2002 after three years of academic improvement begun in 1999. What is even more significant is that the incoming principal, Dr. Gabriela Mafi, with the same group of committed teachers, sustained and increased Rosita's student achievement between 2002 and 2005. From 2005 to the present, a strong district structure and committed teachers have continued to sustain Rosita's high-achieving culture, even after Mafi left the school. When a high-achieving culture is built through dramatic and systemic changes set in motion by a skilled principal and a new principal recognizes and enables that culture to continue to develop, student achievement is sustained and continues to improve.

> When a high-achieving culture is built through dramatic and systemic changes set in motion by a skilled principal and a new principal recognizes and enables that culture to continue to develop, student achievement is sustained and continues to improve.

Dr. Sherry Franklin, Garden Grove Unified School District's Assistant Superintendent of Elementary Education, commented that the placement of principals at Rosita and other elementary schools is the result an "artful" matching of the skills of a principal with the culture of the school and a highly "scaffolded structure" of support that is first and foremost modeled by the collaborative leadership team at the district office. In Garden Grove, there is a prevailing high-achieving culture developed by a visionary and hands-on superintendent, Dr. Laura Schwalm, that "people make a difference" and there is a deliberate effort to cultivate the strengths of principals, teachers, and staff at every level. Collective strengths of all staff are focused by the district leadership team toward high expectations for all students, an ethical framework for decisions—"What is best for students and staff"—and purposeful work within a team (school or district). This cooperative and collaborative spirit has eliminated the need for competition among schools vying for the district's attention. This philosophy in action earned Garden Grove Unified School District the National Broad Award for Urban Education, honoring the most outstanding urban school systems in America, for 2004.

Both Kathy Roe and Gabriela Mafi personify leaders who are passionate in articulating a vision that "all Rosita students can achieve" in alignment with the district vision. "I have worked to keep the vision alive that our students can achieve," said Kathy Roe. "I never ever want to hear that a child can't." Dr. Mafi has also taken up the gauntlet of believing that all of Rosita's children can be successful. "I talked about my experiences as a Mexican American growing up in urban South Los Angeles. I talked about the struggles and what families go through. It was very personal for me," Dr. Mafi shared. She meets with teachers three times each year to review the progress of every child. "Some may

We cannot have double standards for different groups of students. Expecting one thing from, for example, a Vietnamese student and not expecting the same thing from a Latino student, solely on the basis of ethnicity, is not OK."

believe that a certain level of work is all a child is capable of doing in school. But how do we know that? Is it OK if a given student is not doing his work? How do you know that he or she *can't* do that? Are we getting 100 percent effort here? Each and every child must put in 100 percent effort. We cannot have double standards for different groups of students. Expecting one thing from, for example, a Vietnamese student and not expecting the same thing from a Latino student, solely on the basis of ethnicity, is not OK."

Both principals focused immediately on developing leadership and collaboration within the staff, recognizing that empowering teachers is one of the keys to developing a high-achieving culture. Kathy Roe first began the reform process at Rosita to create a team of teachers with a passion and belief that students could be successful and to build a positive attitude about learning with teachers and every staff member of the school community. She commented, "Teachers were working hard but not well together." One Rosita teacher commented, "We really had to look at our instruction. What we were doing was not working."

Consequently, the energies of staff were going in many directions rather than a focused unified direction toward improved student achievement. She began to create a team process that involved organizing grade-level meetings in which she led teachers in the beginning to focus on language arts with the large English-learner population. In structured grade-level meetings, teachers worked and planned together, collaboratively looking at the language arts standards within the grade level and vertically (K–6). In the beginning, teachers shared, it was not always easy. "We had to give up our sacred cows," one teacher stated, indicating how Rosita teachers learned to work as a team. Additionally, teachers said that before they began to base their teaching on the standards, there was little clarity as to what was really important. Preparing for the high-stakes test was a guessing game. As a result of coordinating their instruction and clarifying their grade-level targets, a clear pathway for teaching emerged and student achievement improved.

Kathy focused staff on strategic reading strategies that "worked" and that were verified by research. One of the first strategies she emphasized was direct instruction (DI), both whole and small group, of structured phonics and phonemic awareness for Grades K–3. According to *Direct Instruction* by Engelmann (1980), DI is a model for teaching that emphasizes well-developed and carefully planned lessons designed around students incrementally mastering learning objectives. Whole language, a philosophy that grew out of Noam Chomsky's conception of linguistic development through a natural process, promoted in California during the

1980s and 1990s, did not emphasize a specific structured learning trajectory. Hence, explicit phonics instruction was often left out of early reading instruction. Grades 4 to 6 included a emphasis on core literature to develop reading comprehension and writing rather than comprehension skills that were explicitly taught. DI was integrated into instructional practice at every grade level, with effectiveness checked by running records during the year. In the running record assessment, teachers listen to students read a grade-level passage, record the errors in decoding, and note the student's fluency and comprehension. Based on running record assessment results, every child was placed in small-group reading by level.

Roe then moved teachers into grade-level leadership, guiding them to use individual assessment data to align curriculum and instruction for every student to the standards. In 1999, the published language arts curriculum was not yet aligned completely to the California standards. As grade levels began to use the standards, teachers began to understand what was important to teach rather than to depend on favorite units of instruction that had little alignment with the standards. Teachers began to intervene early when students fell behind or failed to master critical skills. These interventions within the classroom, as well as before and after school, were implemented to address students shown by assessment to be below grade-level expectations. For example, first-grade students who missed specific phonics skills taught during a specific week were immediately scheduled into intervention classes before school the next week, where the skills were retaught and reinforced. The key to intervening with Rosita students was immediacy.

Many schools that structure interventions do not immediately intervene based on what assessments reveal about the students. Interventions often become generalized where teachers know that students have problems but they fail to pinpoint the exact problems and then address those. Other interventions put into place included schoolwide reading goals using the Accelerated Reader Program from Renaissance Learning, manned by a veteran teacher, and an after-school homework club to help students with homework. Accelerated Reader is a program that pinpoints a student's reading level, provides a list of leveled books to read based on the diagnosed level, and assesses comprehension after the student has read each book.

In 2002, when Dr. Mafi arrived, she wisely built on the grade-level structure established by Kathy Roe and provided important validation to the staff of the three years of sustained student achievement. An unskilled principal might have diminished or slowed Rosita's improvement. Sustaining achievement with a different leader when a successful principal leaves is often not thought out by districts. Principal positions are at times politicized without consideration of sustaining student achievement. Dr. Mafi proved to be a wise choice for Rosita by Garden Grove School District because she embraced what the prior principal and teachers had begun. This kind of attitude is unique among leaders, who often come into schools with bulging egos and desires for accolades and who attempt to "steamroll" a successful culture. "I don't think the staff realized how successful they were," said Dr. Mafi. "They thought they were doing OK. At the end of my first year, when we received the California Title I Achieving School Award, they started really believing that they were a high-achieving school." Dr. Mafi further commented that the staff and parent perception of Rosita's success has now changed with three Title 1 Achieving Schools Awards (2002, 2003, and 2004) and a Distinguished School Honorable Mention in 2004, in addition to the Eli Broad Award for the district. Rosita also attained the Distinguished School Award in 2006.

She also helped teachers focus on "next steps" in taking them to the next level of success. This perspective, again, is unique because principals coming in often try to compete with a previous principal's success rather than build on it. She commented that helping teachers take "next steps" rather than looking at "weaknesses" was an important mental adjustment for teachers. As a leader, knowing what is the right step to take with a school is often more important than implementing the change.

The important next steps proved to be emphasizing individual student learning in the classroom, getting parents and students more involved and responsible for student learning, and doing more in-depth analysis of student data. "I saw this as one of the next steps—to raise student awareness of what they were doing and parent awareness of what students were doing." This awareness was accomplished through the creation and implementation of a home-school compact that articulated each stakeholder's responsibilities, as well as behavioral and academic contracts signed daily by the teacher and the parent and weekly by the principal. The compact, which is a requirement of Title 1 schools, is extremely important at Rosita. Unlike many Title 1 schools where the compact is a task to be checked off, at Rosita it is actively and repeatedly emphasized throughout the year with parents and students. Dr. Mafi meets weekly with both students and parents to review student assessments, resolve problems, and enlist parent support for achievement and behavioral goals. She uses the home-school compact as a powerful intervention tool to enlist the support of parents and teachers to alter events affecting student learning. In these meetings, the responsibilities of each stakeholder are spelled out for behavior and academics. As one teacher put it, "Mafi knows every single child at Rosita and has talked with their families." When children successfully complete their contracts or show marked improvement, Mafi sings the Rosita song to them and uses many other positive rewards.

Another next step was developing a more prescriptive and differentiated approach to intervening with students. Teachers were working with students with many differing language arts or math needs solely within their classrooms. There was no prescriptive grouping of students across grade levels based on student assessment analyses. For example, teachers often would be intervening with students who needed basic phonics instruction at the same time as with students who needed specific help in comprehension skills. Dr. Mafi orga-nized intervention across grade levels by the prescriptive needs of students such that students were grouped based on their phonics instruction, fluency, or comprehension needs. "The smaller the pool of the students [in classrooms alone], the less differentiated [the student prescription] will be, the less you are going to be targeting [student] needs." This was another important adjustment that needed to be accomplished to yield improved student achievement. Sustaining schools are those that do not settle for present suc-cess but are always refining and making the necessary improvements to achieve even greater success.

> Sustaining schools are those that do not settle for present success but are always refining and making the necessary improvements to achieve even greater success.

EMPOWERING STAFF TO DO THEIR BEST WORK

Empowering the teaching staff is another secret of Rosita's sustaining suc-cess. Each of Rosita's principals played a critical role in helping teachers become successful. Former principal Kathy Roe commented that it took three years of rapport building with the "right" staff to build positive momentum for student success. Along the way, some teachers came, others rededicated themselves, and others left in the process of sifting out those teachers with a passion for student success from those who did not want to be at Rosita. "We really had to look at our instruction because it wasn't working," one veteran teacher commented. "We were underesti-mating our students—they were more capable of better work."

Roe developed teacher efficacy by weaving research-based reading strategies effective for students into staff development, as well as her classroom observations and teacher evaluations. One of the areas she par-ticularly looked at across all grades was whole-group and small-group direct instruction in the classroom. She observed the implementation of this and other effective strategies by regu-lar classroom visitations, providing consistent feedback to teachers. She would also often eat lunch with staff to listen and to be accessible: "It was just as important to find out those who

> "It was just as important to find out those who were hindering the school improvement process and work with them as well as other highly motivated teachers. Most principals forget that you must work with all teachers."

were hindering the school improvement process and work with them as well as other highly motivated teachers. Most principals forget that you must work with all teachers."

A strategy for empowerment was the grade-level meeting and planning structure that enabled teachers to begin working collaboratively. Teachers of all grade levels commented that the success at Rosita was not due to the efforts of any one teacher but to a team of teachers working together. Kathy Roe began by facilitating every grade level to solve student achievement problems. "There was always a way to solve problems," Kathy commented. "I wanted to get teachers to think about how to solve student achievement problems themselves and to make less of the barriers they saw." Involving teachers in problem solving fostered solutions to student achievement and valuing of teacher input.

Veteran Rosita teachers spoke of a change in mind-set that occurred during the second or third year following their identification as underperforming. One teacher explained, "We changed our mind from we will do what we can for our learners to we will do whatever it takes to help students achieve." This teacher also admitted that, prior to the changes brought on by Rosita's underperforming label, her expectations were not high enough for students. She had many questions: "Will the students change? Will this work?" After the second year and seeing the results of the state tests, this same teacher with the results still in her hands ran to a fellow teacher saying, "I can't believe that what we are building is working." The results built confidence in Rosita teachers. They now knew how to get the job done.

> "We changed our mind from we will do what we can for our learners to we will do whatever it takes to help students achieve."

After Roe's departure, Dr. Mafi expanded the leadership team structure across all grade levels, K–6. Knowing that the staff must take the next steps to increasing student achievement, she commented, "There is a way that you can work people toward the means and ends you want without dictating it. During my very first leadership team meeting, I told the team that we were going to come to consensus on school decisions—we are going to do this together." Several teachers verified that Mafi includes them in school decisions and supports them in the implementation. Dr. Mafi meets with the leadership team formally once or twice monthly with an agenda. She brings draft proposals to the leadership meetings. "I always bring a draft with ideas already on it and then we discuss it and move it forward—this provides a framework and sets them up so that they will be in the chain of power to act as a grade-level chair rather than just being my mouthpiece." Mafi then documents and communicates the leadership team process through structured agendas with action items, information items, and meeting minutes.

Each grade-level chair then meets with grade-level teachers using a structured agenda and action and information items from the leadership team meeting. Teachers at each grade level discuss these items and make written recommendations for next steps, which are given to Dr. Mafi and discussed at the next leadership meeting. "We have a voice and what we say is heard," Rosita teachers commented. Dr. Mafi will, at times, sit in on grade-level meetings to help the meeting go forward, especially if certain grade levels are having difficulty working together. Consensus decisions and further planning for these decisions are brought forward to staff meetings held monthly. Thus, staff meetings are productive and meaningful because all staff have had input prior to the meeting. Dr. Mafi adheres to the philosophy that "staff meetings are a time for purposeful collaboration; they are not a time for me to read aloud things that could be read independently or for us to bicker over small points or procedures that do not affect student learning."

In 2003, Mafi implemented individual teacher meetings three times during the year to review the progress of individual students. Each fall, winter, and spring, five to six days of roving substitutes are provided to release teachers to meet individually for one to two hours with her. During that time, the two review and discuss formative student data, determine needed interventions and then follow-up on the progress of those interventions, and review subsequent benchmark assessments. Through these meetings, she has been able to determine with the teacher what students are doing rather than what the teacher is doing right or wrong. She commented, "The focus is on the student learning outcome. Is this specific strategy or approach reaching the students—and how will we each have to adapt what we are doing to reach all students?" For example, Mafi said, "In one of my meetings, a teacher shared that a certain student was not getting his work done. I suggested starting an academic contract. The teacher commented that she didn't believe that contracts were effective. Since she had never before initiated an academic contract, she couldn't really speak to whether they were working. So, I asked her to humor me and try it. After the fifth week of the contract, the student was completing homework and had met his Accelerated Reader goals. The teacher just told me that she couldn't believe the difference. It's that belief that a child can do it that empowers her!"

ROSITA'S NONNEGOTIABLE CORE VALUES

There are two guiding nonnegotiable core values at Rosita on which both teachers and Mafi agree.

1. **We believe that all students can achieve.** "Our kids can do it! We are going to give them the support, but we are going to make them work their hardest—they do not have a choice. If students aren't working as hard as they possibly can, I am not satisfied because I know that these kids will eventually have to compete with other

> "Our kids can do it! We are going to give them the support, but we are going to make them work their hardest—they do not have a choice. If students aren't working as hard as they possibly can, I am not satisfied because I know that these kids will eventually have to compete with other students for whom English is their first language. So-so is never good enough."

students for whom English is their first language. So-so is never good enough," said Mafi. Rosita teachers commented that in the beginning their expectations were not high enough because of the barriers they saw, such as many limited English students. This perception changed when teachers began to use data and research-based instructional strategies to improve their instruction. They saw that these changes worked and students began to excel, confirming for teachers that Rosita students can indeed achieve.

2. **We expect no less than 100 percent from anyone.** Dr. Mafi and Rosita teachers have shown that they are committed to doing whatever is necessary to get the job done. They often spend ten or more hours a day preparing, meeting, and instructing at the school site. "I take on as much as I can and stay late so that I can be accessible," said Dr. Mafi. "My door is always open to anyone who comes in with anything. I will always work with them to find them an answer." One teacher commented, "I don't mind putting in the hours when Mafi puts in more hours than I do."

ADVICE TO PRINCIPALS

Several important practices from Rosita's principal would benefit any principal desiring to create a high-achieving school.

- **Know each student's name and communicate regularly with parents.** "It is critical to know the students; know where they are academically; know where they are behaviorally and motivationally by being in the classrooms to see where they are. Know the kids from the heart, not just knowing them academically—that you care about them and you want the parents to know that also. My goal at the end of my time here is to know every child's name. I am about two-thirds of the way there. A parent's job is to produce a child who is a good citizen. Our parents are excellent parents who love their children dearly, but they are not experienced, trained teachers. Without explicit directions, parents don't know how to best help their children with their homework or

> "Know the kids from the heart, not just knowing them academically—that you care about them and you want the parents to know that also."

reading comprehension. Our job is to teach our students all of the academics and explicitly inform the parents how they can best support us. We do this through parent education, as well as our weekly Rosita Report, which goes home every Tuesday in our 'Take Home Tuesday' folder. In this newsletter, printed in all three home languages, I provide specific information on how to help students at home with various academic issues, as well as information on what we are doing and why."

- **Believe that the kids can "do it" and keep stressing that with staff.** Mafi often uses herself as an example. "What if no one had believed in me? Where would I be? When given support, students can achieve at increasingly high levels. Their racial or language backgrounds cannot be excuses. We are going to continue to fight lower expectations for high-poverty groups."

- **Celebrate your success along the way.** Teachers, students, staff, and parents must celebrate their academic success. From the Rosita song that is sung each month during Spirit Assemblies celebrating the Students of the Month, to the welcoming, family atmosphere and chocolate pie in the staff room, it is obvious that success is celebrated. "All parents, students, and staff know that there is something so special about Rosita that makes it worth caring and fighting for. When we look at our students, we are looking into the faces of our country's future leaders. No one can tell our students or us that because of their poverty, their nation of origin, or the language they speak at home, they can't do everything that any other child in this state can—even better! Rosita students are winners and we all know it!"

SUSTAINING PROCESSES AT ROSITA

Sustaining processes at work at Rosita to make it a high-performing school include the following:

1. Articulate the vision and passion for student achievement. First and foremost, the principal is consistently articulating the vision and passion for student achievement by focusing and refocusing staff on the belief that students can achieve. Dr. Mafi stresses with everyone—staff, students, and parents—that students can "do it." "I grew up in urban South Los Angeles. Most teachers grow up in middle-class backgrounds. For many of them it is a culture shock to see students that live differently. Often they can make assumptions about students and parents that are erroneous," said Mafi. She has set a goal with staff to achieve 801 for the API. As an expression of this belief, the leadership team is planning to print t-shirts with *801* to keep the dream alive for staff as they stretch toward this new achievement mark.

2. Involve staff in decisions. A collaborative decision-making structure serves to address the "Rosita Single Plan for Student Achievement" by promoting continuous growth and refinement. The application of this structure is directly dependent on the principal organizing and leading staff through the many decisions that must be made to channel staff energy to student success. The process starts with the principal meeting with a representative leadership team (K–6) to build consensus for proposed actions. Grade-level leaders then take proposed actions from the leadership team to a grade-level meeting.

In these meetings, a wider consensus on the action and formation items is achieved with all teachers. After grade-level discussions, proposed decisions and actions are shared back to the principal once again. Finally the proposed action steps are formalized and taken to the entire staff, where plans are made for implementation.

Mafi implemented a two-hour articulation time, once each month, when she met with teachers to analyze data, provide staff development, and do targeted planning. This is built into the school day by hiring substitutes to release the entire grade level for two hours. An example of one activity was to compare the California Standards Test (CST) student scores to the English language arts writing standards to improve the instruction of writing across all grade levels.

3. Analyze student data throughout the year. There is ongoing data analysis of student assessments. In September of the new school year, Mafi guides teachers through a data analysis of the CST, examining student scores in English language arts and mathematics. Teachers identify trends and areas of weakness in instruction by looking at the data of current students and students from the year before. Based on this information, students are grouped according to their test band (Far Below Basic, Below Basic, Basic, Proficient, and Advanced). Teachers look deeper into the data to determine where students scored within the band (bottom, middle, top) and then chart their own students. Mafi also guides teachers in comparing these test scores to the level of student engagement—rebelliousness, retreatism, passive compliance, ritual engagement, and authentic engagement—so that students can be targeted with engagement interventions—close proximity to speaker, corrective feedback, public praise, or academic contract (Brewster & Fager, 2000). Comparing student engagement behavior to their CST scores is a unique practice at Rosita. However, Mafi's quest since she arrived is that students develop responsibility for their own learning. Shaping student engagement behavior is a way to develop independent learners. She tells new students when they arrive, "This is our school. It might be different than the school

> "This is our school. It might be different than the school you went to before and we expect a lot of you. You may have more work than you used to, and you'll have to read every night, including weekends."

you went to before and we expect a lot of you. You may have more work than you used to, and you'll have to read every night, including weekends."

Throughout the year, a Web-based multiple-measures student assessment system called Data Director, developed by Garden Grove Unified School District, is used along with curricular assessments to monitor student progress in language arts and mathematics. Assessments are entered quarterly into the Web-based system to provide individual, classroom, and disaggregated groups information. Reports can be generated quickly from this system. Dr. Mafi then meets with teachers three times during the year in student study teams to review the testing data for every student. She meets with each teacher about every child in the classroom. "I have all the data from a schoolwide perspective. I go over individual student data, and then we can use these results for reteaching, grouping, and intervention." Students are grouped within the classroom, depending on the kind of readers they are and based on their fluency and comprehension scores on assessments—automatic word callers, struggling word callers, word stumblers, slow and steady comprehenders, slow word callers, or disabled readers (Buly & Valencia, 2003). A credentialed and trained long-term substitute is also employed at the school from October through the end of April. She works with various grade levels throughout the day to provide small group intervention at all grade levels to meet the needs of struggling readers in upper grades. She works directly with Mafi to create the schedule, determine the curriculum and pacing, and monitor ongoing student progress.

4. Hold targeted and timely interventions with struggling students. Prescriptive intervention is definitely a sustaining process at Rosita. Teachers moved from "doing their own intervention" to "targeted" intervention with more in-depth data analysis with Dr. Mafi. "What I do is sit with teachers and go over all student reading levels. I take out their leveled reading passages (running records) and if they are below grade level, we write down what type of reader they are. We disaggregate accuracy, fluency, and comprehension and determine the student's relative strengths and weaknesses, as well as next steps for assessment and instruction. After meetings with all teachers in the grade level, I group all students in a given grade level by specific need—disabled readers with phonemic awareness skills, automatic word callers with comprehension strategies, etc."

From these individual meetings with teachers, the principal builds an intervention list of students according to their specific reading needs. After-school intervention classes twice weekly are organized during the fall and winter months based on targeted reading needs of students. Grade-level teachers are paid extra to teach intervention classes for these prescriptive groups. These teachers agree on the effective strategies and use the district-approved intervention programs. Teachers do not "do their own thing" during targeted intervention. Student learning in after-school intervention classes is monitored and adjusted through the regular ongoing assessments during the year.

5. Use academic contracts. A fifth sustaining process is the strategic use of academic contracts with students and parents. This practice stems from students not meeting the expectations articulated in the home-school compact signed at the beginning of the year. This compact articulates five actions that each stakeholder (students, parents, teachers, and office staff) agrees to take. For students these actions include (1) attitude: coming to school on time with a positive attitude prepared to be responsible and active learners; (2) class work: paying attention, following directions, and participating actively, giving 100 percent effort; (3) homework: completing and returning homework on time; (4) rules: following school and class-room rules at all times, demonstrating respect for self and others; and (5) daily practice: reading daily at home for fifteen to thirty minutes and prac-ticing math facts daily. Students are reminded of the compact frequently—at each assembly and every possible opportunity. Rosita's home-school compact is featured in Figure 5.1.

"I saw when I arrived that students weren't holding themselves accountable for what they were doing in school, so we enacted academic contracts," said Mafi. Any student who demonstrates poor effort, engage-ment, work habits, or attitudes toward school will have an academic con-tract initiated with specific behavioral improvements that must be made. These improvements could be "listening to directions, getting started immediately, completing or submitting all homework on time with the best effort," or others. Mafi conducts the initial meetings in which the teacher, parents, and child are present. The teacher explains the concerns related to the student, and Dr. Mafi explains the contract process and pur-pose, as well as each stakeholder's responsibility. The academic difficulties that a student is experiencing are discussed and a contract is developed that the teacher fills out daily and sends home. The parent provides mutu-ally agreed-on consequences, positive or negative, depending on the day's report.

At these meetings, Mafi stresses with students and parents the impor-tance of hard work and good grades. "I explain why this is so important to our parents in Spanish. I am the fifth of six children. I know that our immigrant parents are working themselves ragged to create the best life and opportunities for their children. Their children are their hope for the future. Often, the students don't appreciate the hard work and sacrifice of their parents; they'd rather watch *The Simpsons* than study. The parents say to their children, 'I didn't have the chance to go to college in Mexico. I have to work. I want you to have an easier life and not have to work so hard.' I explain to students and parents that college is free (financial aid) for students who do well in school. I have the students visualize the type of future they want and the comforts that hard work and an education will provide. I remind the students that, one day, they will be caring for their parents. How to pay back their own parents for all of the hard work and sacrifice? By their own hard work!"

Figure 5.1 Rosita Home-School Compact: 2004–2005

Student: _____ Room: _____ Teacher: _____

Students will...	Parents will...	Teachers will...	The Office Staff will...
Attitude:			
1. (a) Come to school on time daily with a positive attitude; (b) be prepared to be responsible, motivated, and active learners who demonstrate pride in themselves and school.	1. Ensure that children are ready to learn at school: well-rested, fed, well-groomed, and have school materials as needed.	1. Provide quality teaching and leadership to students and families, a positive safe environment, and a variety of teaching strategies to meet student needs. Provide opportunities for all students to learn.	1. Provide support for communication with families, both written and verbal, with quick responses. Provide parents with support contacts; allow parents to feel comfortable in calling or visiting school.
Class work:			
2. In class: pay attention and listen, follow directions and participate actively, giving 100 percent effort, best quality, and neat work daily. Ask questions and get help when needed.	2. Check papers, textbooks, and other materials sent home to know what your child is learning. Maintain open line of communication between self, students, and school to check on students' progress frequently. Attend all conferences and school functions, as well as requesting additional conferences as needed.	2. Assign homework that reinforces skills taught in school. Hold students accountable for every assignment.	2. Support teachers with issues related to discipline, truancy, tardiness, supplies, equipment, curriculum, training, and positive reinforcement. Eliminate unnecessary paperwork.
Homework:			
3. Complete and return homework on time, having	3. Ensure a time and place for students to complete homework.	3. Be available to parents and students to provide extra	3. Welcome and involve all families. Provide a folder

(Continued)

Figure 5.1 (Continued)

Students will...	Parents will...	Teachers will...	The Office Staff will...
made best (100 percent) effort (including neatness) with parent signature if requested.	Take initiative to pick up (or arrange for pickup of) student work when children are absent.	support whenever possible. Communicate frequently and consistently with families about students' academics and behavior and teacher expectations through conferences, phone calls, and notes home.	(Take Home Tuesday) for students to take home important papers one day a week that is known by parents. Post flyers for parents to readily see.
Rules: 4. Follow school and classroom rules at all times, including demonstrating respect for self and others (adults and students).	4. Communication from teacher and/or school is read and (if required) signed and returned promptly. Provide positive or negative reinforcement at home, as necessary, to support classroom teachers. Encourage and maintain positive attitudes toward school.	4. Maintain consistent academic and behavioral standards for students.	4. Provide follow-through and support between teachers and home (calls, absences, tardies, etc.).
Daily Practice: 5. Read daily at home for fifteen to thirty minutes (minimum) and practice math facts daily.	5. Ensure that child has a library card and is trained to use library and available resources; seek out academic support for child. Ensure that child reads at home daily.	5. Keep up with current educational techniques/issues; continue professional growth as educator.	5. Provide parents with specific strategies to enhance education of all students.
Student signature:	**Parent signature:**	**Teacher signature:**	**Administrator signature:**

On Fridays, Dr. Mafi signs the academic contract. Dr. Mafi then personally keeps track of each contract (along with the teacher) and celebrates the improvement in effort and work habits with students by singing them songs (to the tune of "Oh, Mickey, You're So Fine," inserting the student's name) and giving praise to reinforce the changes. To provide added motivation, teachers commented that when a child is close to achieving, Mafi brings the student in to "smell the candy" he or she will receive when he or she meets their contract goal. Dr. Mafi has a personal vested interest in the success of these students and considers them "smaller versions of herself" with challenges similar to those she faced.

6. Provide staff encouragement and validation. A sixth sustaining process is consistently validating and encouraging the efforts of staff. Mafi prefaces every new idea with "We are doing a great job" and all next steps with "It is threatening but we always have to get better at what we do. Let's celebrate what we are doing now and then look at new ideas." She is constantly reading the emotional state of staff as she leads staff to greater success with students. Key teachers come to her when staff are stressed or overwhelmed. She is wise enough to pull back to give the staff a break. "I've been at some schools where there have been great ideas but everyone got burned out." Her teachers verify that she takes the time to celebrate and laugh with them. She is highly visible around the campus and makes herself available throughout the day to address any need that a teacher, student, or parent may have. Teachers also reported that "staff needs are addressed immediately."

Since she arrived, Mafi has concentrated on securing community and state validation of Rosita's success. Rosita received a third Title 1 Achieving School Award (2002, 2003, and 2004) for the impressive growth of students meeting or exceeding state standards. The school was in the final visitation for the 2005 California Distinguished School Award. Mafi plans to lead the school to higher levels of success, refusing to allow poverty and language proficiency to prevent any student from achieving mastery—and of course celebrating along the way.

LESSONS LEARNED FROM ROSITA ELEMENTARY SCHOOL

A well-defined structure "clarifies" the mission of the school from the district on down. High levels of trust are in place between the school and the district office, and between the district office and the school.

There is lock-step implementation in language arts and math. An infrastructure of accountability within the school occurs through a designated leadership team, grade-level structure, and principal-teacher interactions.

Grade-level leaders take the responsibility to orient new teachers. Each teacher meets with the principal three times during the year to review every student's data and determine next steps with these students. In addition, there is structured articulation of curriculum and instruction among all grade levels.

Home-school compacts are taken seriously. Students are put on academic contracts whenever they are having difficulty in the classroom. The compact, which is developed between the student, parent, and teacher, monitors attitude, class work, homework, following school rules, and daily reading. The contract, which is monitored weekly, remains in place until the student demonstrates improvement in learning. At that time the student is taken off the contract and receives rewards.

"We [teachers] changed our mind from we will do what we can for our learners to we will do whatever it takes to help students achieve."

6

Baldwin Elementary School, Alhambra, California

A Culture of High Expectations

Martha Baldwin Elementary School, named for a woman who took it upon herself to make sure the children in that area had enough food to eat, now makes sure that children have the best educational opportunities possible. As articulated in their California Distinguished Schools application, this K–8 school and its community made it their mission to empower students to become "self-motivators, observers, investigators, high-level thinkers, effective communicators, problem solvers, risk takers, collaborative workers and culturally literate." As a result, Baldwin is a rare "triple crown" school in California—Title 1 Achieving School 2002–2006, California Distinguished School 2002 and 2006, and National Blue Ribbon School 2003. Baldwin has also received the Governor's Performance Award 2000–2003. These are remarkable achievements for a K–8 school with the challenge that middle-school students present.

Immediately, I noted Baldwin's pride in the school. Painted on the front of the building for all to see was the emblem of its National Blue Ribbon

Table 6.1   API Scores for Baldwin Elementary School

Year	1999	2000	2001	2002	2003	2004	2005	Seven-Year Growth
Schoolwide API	670	689	720	742	755	773	787	117
Asian Subgroup API	756	781	807	802	814	825	837	81
Latino Subgroup API	512	531	571	625	638	664	678	166
SED API	639	662	702	723	739	746	768	129

Award. Even with their obvious repeated successes and many academic awards, I found the faculty and staff to be warm and inviting. One cannot help but feel a positive energy and the beat of a purposeful agenda exhibited by every staff member within the school. At Baldwin, a relentless pursuit of high academic achievement is shared by every staff member.

Baldwin belongs to the select group of Title 1 schools that have sustained student achievement for more than five years. However, as with many of the high-performing Title 1 schools, a sustaining pattern of achievement has been in place for some time. This pattern is evident over the past twelve years at Baldwin. For as long as the Academic Performance Index (API) has been calculated in California, Baldwin has grown from an API of 670 to 815 today. In 1999, a 244-point gap occurred between the Hispanic subgroup and the Asian subgroup. The number of Baldwin Caucasian students is not high enough to be considered significant. There was also a 117-point gap between the socio-economically disadvantaged (SED) subgroup and that same Asian subgroup. The gaps between these subgroups have been significantly reduced over seven years to 159 and 69, respectively (see Table 6.1). I've found this is common with schools that have established a high-achieving culture. Once this culture has been realized at a school, achievement continually improves. This pattern of achievement at Baldwin is shown in Table 6.1.

BUILDING A HIGH-ACHIEVING CULTURE

The creation and development of a high-achieving culture are purposefully brought about by the leadership of the principal. Any new principal coming into a low-performing school must first identify with the existing culture and then sensitively and positively work with all aspects of the school community—teachers, parents, and students—to transform the low-achieving mind-set to one of high achievement. At Baldwin, the principal proceeded to win the hearts of her staff and rallied them to declare war on low student achievement.

Important First Steps

Twelve years ago, the standardized test scores at Baldwin had reached a plateau and student achievement was declining. It was at this time that Liz Ramos Hanacek became Baldwin's principal. Dr. Liz Hanacek is a high-energy, positive, "no nonsense" principal who "speaks from her heart," as one of her leadership team characterized her. She has a never-ending determination and perseverance to make Baldwin a great school through a unified team effort, without alienating her teachers. "She treats us like human beings and doesn't talk down to us," reported her leadership team. Hanacek understands her role as the chief administrator and knows how to lead her staff to achieve a great mission.

In addition to being eminently qualified, she had unique preparation prior to coming to Baldwin. She was asked by her husband, a successful businessman, "What are you going to do to make a difference at that school?" She initially told him at the time that she would make sure the students were learning and that they felt safe and secure. Her husband pressed her further, "But how are you going to prove it or show it?"

"We will see it on their faces and in the atmosphere of the school," she responded. He persisted, "No, what is going to be your concrete evidence? There has got to be concrete evidence at that school."

She replied, "Well, I guess it has to be the test scores. My evidence will be improved test scores." She also inherently knew that she needed to influence staff to get them "on the same page" with this mission. She religiously influenced her staff to share the same determination, demand for success, and energy required to attack student achievement at Baldwin.

Hanacek came to Baldwin with a commitment to using achievement data as a verification of success long before data were taken seriously by most principals. She understood that to make a difference in the lives of students, achievement had to improve, and that achievement would verify the school's success. This clarity of purpose is not commonly found at a low-achieving school where often low achievement is allowed to be politicized and rationalized. Little did she know that improving student achievement data would also improve the performance of teachers, encourage students and parents, and break the mold of the unsuccessful pattern commonly seen at Title 1 schools.

Hanacek began her attack on student performance with an all-out effort to create a shared vision for achievement. This is the most important place for a principal to begin. However, a leader cannot force teachers to share a vision. Teachers must be led to this vision by a principal they trust. Baldwin teachers had lost sight of a shared purpose for their work. They had become isolated, doing their own independent "thing." Principals coming to low-achieving schools must reclaim the belief that all students can learn and that teachers can be effective even with the most difficult students. Teachers in low-achieving schools subconsciously embrace low expectations of students, making faulty assumptions based on perceived or real failure. Thus, Hanacek was certain that everyone had to be on the same page and that she had to move them away from their isolated practice to one of a collaborative practice. Because Hanacek knew Baldwin teachers were very good teachers, she deliberately set about to resurrect the vision of high expectations for student achievement.

Effective principals always build on the positives rather than the negatives. Among many school administrators, there is a misguided notion that a leader can "boss" or mandate staff to perform better. Under these circumstances, the staff will comply marginally but hardly ever perform at a high level. A principal must first recognize and affirm the strengths in the staff to create teamwork and camaraderie. Then, the principal working collaboratively with teachers will be able to address weaknesses that prevent students from achieving.

Building on the positives, Hanacek visited classrooms at every opportunity, interacting with teachers daily and expressing confidence in them on a regular basis. She also was determined to create a warm and supportive work environment. Second to creating a student achievement vision was her goal of "making teachers happy," yet never losing sight of what the ultimate target was. "I didn't come in as a strong change agent in the beginning. I was going to make sure I gained their trust. I spent the first one and a half years making friends with them—celebrating their accomplishments. I spent a lot of time in classrooms and a lot of time getting buy-in."

It is really so easy for teachers to succumb to low expectations for students and for themselves when principal leadership is absent or weak in the face of all those student achievement challenges. Typically in schools with a weak leader, the principal spends most of his or her time in the office—separated from staff—carrying out what he or she thinks are the important tasks of administration. When principals become separated from their teachers, they extinguish any quality communication or shared focus or high expectations for students. Typically, low expectations are further exacerbated by isolated practice where teachers are cut off from interaction with colleagues and lose sight of the purpose for their work. The result is an organization filled with cranky, frustrated people who devour each other, creating a caustic context for students.

During her second year as principal, after exhaustive and concerted trust building, encouragement, and making friends, Hanacek began working with staff to develop a school vision for high achievement, asking repeatedly, "Where do we want our school to be?" She also recalled articulating her vision, "Someday you will be a distinguished school. You are that good here." The Baldwin teachers resonated with these words, and they began to build a vision together with specific goals; then they set about systematically accomplishing those goals through a shared decision-making process. Baldwin teachers also indicated that the high-achieving culture present at the school evolved over time. They all felt that Hanacek treated them with respect, created a relaxed atmosphere, and built trust with them. "She doesn't talk down to us," one teacher commented. "She took a deliberate approach to build a team here to create buy-in." Teachers in unison commented on the "teacher appreciation barbeque" that Hanacek gives where she flips burgers for staff, as well as other special events she organizes to appreciate staff and encourage fun and camaraderie.

Building a high-achieving culture at a low-performing school depends on a relentless attack by the principal on low expectations. Principals must formulate a "battle plan" as Hanacek did to address the issues behind the low achievement, and yet the battle must be waged as a rallying cry, marshalling staff to come together to overcome the obstacles that prevent students from achieving. To do this, principals must be clear about what they want to do and where they want to take the school. By regularly analyzing student data, principals become clear and focused on what really matters, instead of being drawn into political battles that will divide their focus. In addition to using data strategically, principals must convince, encourage, and strengthen staff daily to believe that the work involved in becoming high achieving is worth the

> By regularly analyzing student data, principals become clear and focused on what really matters, instead of being drawn into political battles that will divide their focus.

effort. From this transformation of low achieving to high achieving emerged Baldwin's nonnegotiable core values that have led to a sustaining pattern of high achievement for more than five years.

BALDWIN'S NONNEGOTIABLE CORE VALUES

The direct result of building a high-achieving culture is the securing of a unity of purpose for one's work captured in core values. Core values center teachers, administrators, classified staff, and parents on a unified mission for high achievement. These values are not merely written down but are emblazoned on the souls of all Baldwin staff. When the everyday stresses of running the "school business" become extremely challenging and exhausting, these values hold the organization together and help to refocus every individual on what matters most—student achievement.

High expectations for students, teachers, and administrators form the heart and soul of core values at Baldwin. These values are fueled by an obviously confident group of successful teachers and administrators who have an unwavering belief in what they can accomplish together. Baldwin's nonnegotiable core values are listed as follows:

1. We believe in high expectations for all students. We don't just believe that certain students can be successful.

2. We are committed to do whatever it takes to help students to be successful.

3. We are committed to learn better ways of teaching and solve challenges we face.

4. We are committed to assisting parents in any way so that children will be supported in learning.

These core values are also the heart and soul of Baldwin's battle plan, and they help to provide the energy and purpose to everything the teachers do to help children succeed.

EMPOWERING THE RIGHT PEOPLE

Great principals know how to articulate a vision and build a superior team of teachers. Great principals also know how to attract teachers who have a passion for helping students be successful and how to help those who are not committed to move on to something else. Great principals also recognize and release the talents of their teachers and mentor them into leadership roles that will support and sustain the organization. Great principals and great teams of teachers transform their schools, producing outstanding student achievement.

Look to the Stronger Teachers

It was clear from the beginning who were the stronger teachers at Baldwin. After all, Hanacek had spent extensive time in classrooms observing teaching and curriculum implementation. She took the critical first step of empowering her strong teachers. A leader must capitalize on the talent within the staff. Principals who maintain a tight control will have a difficult time seeing the talent in their teachers. As a matter of fact, such principals often are threatened by their teachers and will prevent them from filling any meaningful leadership role. But team-building principals release the talents resident in their staff and permit these staff members to become leaders.

The strong teachers at Baldwin did indeed become leaders on the leadership team, and many of them later took other roles in the district or became principals themselves. Hanacek encouraged her teachers from the beginning to assist with staff development, facilitate collaboration, and participate in making decisions. "We are part of a team—collaborating and solving problems. Liz supports us in our decisions. We feel free to really say what we think, even if we don't always agree," articulated the leadership team members. They added, "People are surprised that we have a good relationship with our administrator. This relationship helps us to relax and our children relax because kids know that we work together here."

One strong Baldwin teacher leader is David Byer. Byer was one of these key individuals whom Hanacek empowered to became Baldwin's Title 1 Instructional Specialist seven years ago. Byer, who was a middle-school teacher at Baldwin, has become Baldwin's "data specialist," helping teachers use student assessment strategically to alter curriculum and instruction. Byer, according to Hanacek, is especially effective when it comes to implementing new ideas and assisting teachers. In his own words, he "serves the teachers in whatever needs doing," translating new ideas into action steps, helping teachers to become successful.

> "People are surprised that we have a good relationship with our administrator. This relationship helps us to relax and our children relax because kids know that we work together here."

The Baldwin teachers do feel sufficiently empowered to try any strategy that will help address student learning challenges. They indicated that they felt as if they were "entrepreneurs" in the classroom—supported, respected, and most importantly, successful. "Our success has given us freedom and has provided a springboard to confidence in dealing with new challenges and trying new strategies." These teachers also said that they feel free to express their opinions and to be outspoken, which is rare in struggling schools. Often, the pressure to escape the low-performing label doesn't elicit a positive working relationship between teachers and the principal. At Baldwin, Hanacek has cultivated a belief system with teachers to do anything that it takes to help students become successful and has verified their success through data. "We are like a family—we don't always agree but we are not fearful of criticism. We work as a team to solve problems."

> "Our success has given us freedom and has provided a springboard to confidence in dealing with new challenges and trying new strategies."

Reluctant Staff

Some staff at Baldwin took a little bit longer to change. Other teachers stepped up to help the reluctant teachers change. "It is difficult for some not to accept change when many other teachers were changing," said

Hanacek. She has also allowed teachers to implement instruction in their own way "as long as they were moving in the right direction." Teachers on the leadership team commented that the principal gives them "freedom to choose the strategies they think are best with students." Other team members indicated that they are free to try different strategies to deal with challenges. One leadership team member commented, "We have the freedom to try different approaches to solve learning problems. We have been successful and our success gives us freedom and confidence as we deal with new challenges." Hanacek said, "I believe in keeping people happy; however, when teachers were not able to accept Baldwin's values and their strategies and classroom management were ineffective, we assisted and supported them in a direction that would meet our goals, and we had the support of the district," when referring to times where she had to address teachers who were ineffective.

Through using the No Child Left Behind requirements for highly qualified teachers, the principal was able to make a very strategic move with her middle-school teachers. Because Baldwin is a K–8 school, it is evaluated both as an elementary and a middle school. With the K–5 consistently outperforming Grades 6–8, the leadership team looked for a new middle-school model in 2001. After researching several models, the leadership team recommended a team-teaching model, with one teacher responsible for language arts and history and another teacher responsible for science and math. Some teachers "were clearly uncomfortable with that teaching model." However, that did not stop the plan. These teachers asked for a transfer and it was provided for them. Then Hanacek convinced four of her strong K–1 teachers four years ago to teach at the eighth-grade level. Hanacek commented they were hesitant at first about making that change but because of the level of trust and collaboration she has with her staff, she was able to convince her staff to go forward with it. As a result, Baldwin increased its API by 20 points that year.

This move was strategic for increasing the performance of middle-school students. Hanacek and her teachers were not satisfied with their past efforts to improve student achievement. Yet, she did not stall or become stalemated because of low achievement at the middle school. As a result of this move, Baldwin has grown in API from 713 to now more than 800 at the middle-school grades.

Advice on Empowering Teachers

Empowering and coordinating teachers at Baldwin are key elements in increasing student achievement. Releasing the gifts and talents of these teachers created a powerful and sustaining efficacy that continues to motivate Baldwin teachers to improve their practice. Baldwin teachers I interviewed indicated that they don't teach to receive awards. They take great pride in refining their teaching to better address students they see in their classrooms every day. Teachers can be empowered to achieve a high level of professionalism by the principal in the following ways:

- Getting to know the teachers at a personal level and treating them with respect.
- Building trust through consistently modeling fairness and follow-through.
- Remembering to listen first, speak or advise second.
- Allowing teachers a voice in decision making.
- Mentoring teachers to fill leadership roles.
- Looking for strengths and capitalizing on those strengths.
- Encouraging teachers to perform at the highest level by modeling extraordinary performance.
- Viewing the glass as half-full rather than half-empty—there is great power in optimism.
- Recognizing that challenges are opportunities for collective wisdom.
- Believing that teaching practice that results in increased student achievement brings fulfillment and confidence.

MASTERY OF STANDARDS

Attacking the California standards in instruction was fundamental to Baldwin's assault on low student achievement. The leadership team and principal shared that in the beginning it was difficult to align the state standards to existing curriculum and instruction. Now teachers use the California *Standards Blueprints* and released test questions in a relentless effort to help students master the standards by the end of the year. This focus supports what Hanacek has emphasized: "You can never let your guard down and you must be about always refining your practice so that you can push student achievement even higher."

The mastery of standards is essential to any school's goal of becoming a high-achieving school. *Mastery* refers to the student's ability to demonstrate certain knowledge and skills that are required by that standard. Though curricular materials used in California public schools are standards-aligned, that does not equate to the fact that the content that is actually taught is also standards-aligned. Typically, teachers begin at page one of their standards-

> "You can never let your guard down and you must be about always refining your practice so that you can push student achievement even higher."

aligned text and try to "cover" everything in their book, thereby "satisfying" the standards. Over and over again, I have seen pacing guides that begin at page one of the text and end at the last page of the text. Such an approach lacks the focus that is critical to the essential standards—those frequently assessed. This is especially true with the reading standards for many Title 1 schools. Additionally, ongoing assessments must monitor standards mastery so that teachers can reteach or reinforce immediately those concepts or skills that are weak. Often benchmark assessments of standards collected by schools or districts may not be given to teachers for timely analysis. Thus, teachers probably will not know to what extent specific standards are mastered and which standards still need reinforcing or reteaching. The use of assessments to measure the progress of standards eliminates the guesswork, confirming for teachers what students actually know and can demonstrate.

At Baldwin, Hanacek and the teachers went after all of the standards with a vengeance. They were not satisfied with getting a modest increase in student achievement by addressing some of the standards—they attacked all of the standards. To create momentum across the year, Hanacek feels that the teaching of standards, especially the "pacing" of the standards, is critical and the most difficult process they face. Teachers work from pacing guides that help them focus strategically on the standards across the year. However, the guides are constantly reviewed and adjusted based on how students are learning. Pacing guides do help ensure teachers will adequately address the standards for that grade level during the year. Still, Baldwin takes a more aggressive approach, taking nothing for granted. "Pacing is the scary part now. We are focusing on the essential standards now, but what do we do if we don't get to all of the standards?" is a question that Hanacek and her staff constantly ask themselves. To pinpoint their focus even more, teachers use the California Department of Education's *Standards Blueprints*, which give percentages of questions assigned to standards assessed by the state tests. They also have accessed the sample test questions available.

> At Baldwin, Hanacek and the teachers went after all of the standards with a vengeance. They were not satisfied with getting a modest increase in student achievement by addressing some of the standards—they attacked all of the standards.

Byer has produced standards checklists for teachers so that they can monitor their progress in addressing the standards. Baldwin teachers concentrate on those standards with the greater percentage of test questions. However, Hanacek commented, "We realized this year after looking at how our students performed on the California Standards Test that we must take a look at the other [standards] areas with the lesser percentages. We changed our mind about just concentrating on those standards with the greater percentages. We realized that we can't take anything for granted." Hanacek and other Title 1 principals in high-achieving schools, are realizing that they must continuously refine their school's strategic focus on standards as they approach higher and higher Academic Performance Index scores in order to meet the proficiency requirements of students for the No Child Left Behind legislation.

Another variable that will hinder standards mastery is the lack of exposure to the core curriculum. In greatly affected low-achieving schools, the curriculum is often "dumbed down" to assist students to master the content. For example, when schools split up the seventh-grade prealgebra curriculum into two years instead of exposing all students to the core, research data and experience have shown that students fall even farther behind under the guise of helping students to get caught up. Hanacek firmly believes that students need to be given every chance to be exposed to and challenged by grade-level curriculum. "I am a strong believer that we need to challenge the kids and put them into the curriculum. For example, I wanted all eighth graders to be in algebra with *no* prealgebra. I went back and forth with my teachers on this. If they are all in algebra, there is a much better chance for them to test proficient even though they are not ready." Hanacek makes a good point here that we often hold back students, thinking we are doing them a service by providing more time to master the standards. Instead, we subtly give students the message that they are not capable of mastering algebra or any other curricula.

The leadership team commented that often they have frank discussions about issues such as math instruction, but, when it comes down to it, they indicated that they always ask themselves, "Are we teaching the standards to the level we need to?" Hanacek, with the support of her leadership team, tested her theory with sixth-grade math and found that her students met the challenge, improving from 27 percent proficient to 48 percent proficient when the change was first implemented.

Baldwin staff is realizing that to get to higher and higher levels of achievement, they must continuously declare war on low achievement. Teachers know they must be even more vigilant in how the standards are addressed with their students in effective first teaching. For students who are behind academically, intervention must be more targeted to get at the low-achievement issues quicker. Baldwin is targeting the middle-school grades, particularly the content areas of science and history, where the application of reading and math skills, as well as writing skills, is being measured by the California Standards Tests (CSTs). Proficiency in the content areas is critical to success in high school.

USING STUDENT ACHIEVEMENT DATA

Examining student achievement data is vital and strategic in Baldwin's unfailing pursuit of high academic achievement. State testing data, along with benchmark assessment data collected during the year, are used to provide feedback on student mastery of standards. Hanacek's core philosophy is "never let your guard down" regarding the use of student achievement data. "We cannot compromise student academics at all. We will do what we need to do to help students succeed." Hanacek also does

"We cannot compromise student academics at all. We will do what we need to do to help students succeed."

not wait for district direction regarding the use of achievement data. She and the leadership team take charge of their own improvement process for students right from the beginning.

At the Beginning of the School Year

In all the Alhambra schools, the district spends half a day at each school to review test data taken from the spring testing. Conversations are conducted as to the meaning of the data and initial plans are made for the coming year. The accountability focus is initiated when the entire leadership team participates with Hanacek in an "accountability review." Both the principal and the team members speak highly of this process where the team is introduced to current student achievement data. The team consists of one representative from each grade level, kindergarten through eighth grade, the Resource Specialist, Title 1 Instructional Specialist (David Byer), and Hanacek. Data are comprised of the California Achievement Tests, version 6 (CAT/6), CST, Adequate Yearly Progress (AYP), API, district reading assessments, district writing assessments, district math assessments, results from standards-based report cards, and the California English Language Development Test (CELDT) results from the previous school year. Accountability review documents become working documents that do not remain on the shelf but are used purposefully throughout the year.

At Hanacek's first staff meeting of the year, the leadership team and Byer present the data to the rest of the teachers. Byer provides critical support in helping teachers manage and understand this data. He prepares important current data on each student in language arts and math so that teachers can begin working with students the first day of instruction. Data sheets for each classroom are sorted by CST in math and language arts and ranked from high to low. In this way, the teachers and Hanacek know which students are Far Below Basic, Below Basic, and Basic to target for both in-class and after-school interventions.

After school begins, grade levels meet again to delve deeper into the accountability data and develop priorities for the school year. Baldwin teachers are not resentful or fearful of examining students' achievement data because teachers consider this process as part of their attack strategy. Typically, these beginning grade-level meetings are one-and-one-half hours long after school and are attended by Hanacek and Byer. The CST data, CAT/6, and CELDT levels are analyzed as to what each student needs at each grade level. According to Hanacek, it takes at least one-and-one-half months during the fall for every grade level to meet to establish its instructional battle plan for the year. After the initial grade-level meeting, Hanacek does not attend monthly grade-level meetings except by invitation. She does however create monthly agendas to provide direction to grade levels as they continue their march to high achievement across the year. The results and plans developed at these meetings are communicated to the principal through notes or through personal meetings with the grade-level leader. Based on each grade level's plan, Hanacek prepares the "Baldwin Notebook," which consolidates all the information teachers need about curriculum, instruction, assessment, professional development, discipline, and so on, to propel every teacher toward achieving consistency and high achievement across the school. Hanacek's notebook becomes the battle plan for helping all teachers to be on the same page—providing clarification, urgency, and the mission for everyone to step into his or her very important roles to make student achievement happen during the year.

Tracking Assessments Across the Year

Baldwin teachers use a number of curriculum-based assessments to monitor each student's learning across the year. Byer has the direct responsibility to monitor and manage all use of assessments with teachers and grade levels. Classroom teachers use a portfolio system to document and monitor assessment results. Each student has a prescribed learning plan and is monitored individually. When assessment shows that grade levels or individual teachers need assistance with students, three Title 1 teachers partner with classroom teachers to assist students experiencing difficulties revealed by assessments.

Each student's portfolio contains reading and math assessments, writing assessments, and the English learner profile. Each profile also contains the CELDT results and English-learner levels. These profiles demonstrate for teachers and administrators where students are meeting standards across the year and where students need more support and/or intervention. If students require intervention, Byer works with teachers to schedule students in after-school intervention or homework clubs. At the end of the year, these portfolios are passed from grade to grade so the new teacher can begin where the previous year's teacher left off. As with all effective Title 1 schools, assessment is personalized and monitored student by student. The emphasis is on each student's progress and this progress is measured across the year.

Strategic Intervention

In a number of ways, based on student assessments, Baldwin intervenes with students who are not mastering the standards.

- A schoolwide strategy with the many English learners calls for students to be grouped by language needs, especially in the early grades. For example, first-grade students at the beginning, early intermediate, or intermediate proficiency LEP levels are grouped to better meet their instructional needs.

- Students are grouped within the regular classroom as instruction is differentiated based on the student mastery of specific standards.
- Students identified by state testing and benchmark assessments are recommended to attend an after-school program, three days a week. The program taught by Baldwin teachers primarily focuses on students with a literacy diagnosis, with a secondary emphasis on math.
- For lower achieving students in the middle-school grades, Baldwin uses Scholastic's Read 180 as a Title 1 intervention program within the school day. Students in sixth, seventh, or eighth grades take this class during their elective period. The class is purposefully kept small— with fifteen students, one teacher, and one instructional assistant.
- A homework club is open during the afternoons for students to receive help from teachers. It is a drop-in program that students can access for help with any academic area.

BALDWIN'S SUSTAINING ELEMENTS

The practices that have propelled Baldwin's growth for more than twelve years, establishing a firm foundation and a pattern of sustained achievement, are as follows:

> "Everyone has to be on the same page with achievement. Students know what is expected of them. We all have taken on the challenge of becoming better."

> "We look at each student and where they need to be. We would never do anything different. It has become part of who we are."

- **A collective vision for student achievement.** A vision of high expectations for students guides the work at Baldwin. Teachers, staff, students, parents, and the community share this common vision. They are simply not satisfied with status quo. "Everyone has to be on the same page with achievement. Students know what is expected of them. We all have taken on the challenge of becoming better."

- **Using data to guide continuous improvement.** The data guide Baldwin teachers throughout the year. Data are personalized to each student's progress. "We look at each student and where they need to be. We would never do anything different. It has become part of who we are."

- **Staff pride in raising student achievement.** Baldwin teachers are happy and extremely successful with students. When teachers are successful, the work of teaching doesn't seem hard and there is a great deal of fulfillment as they see students continually improve. The teachers believe "they are the strongest link" and they are confident in knowing that they can deal with *any* student achievement challenges.

Overall, Baldwin is a school community that has a vision of high expectations for students, for teachers, and for the school community. Baldwin teachers and staff are continually refining every aspect of their school practice. They are not satisfied to be just average. Even when administrators and teachers are not applying to be a California Distinguished School, they use the rubric every year to impose those expectations on themselves. They continuously find satisfaction in helping students become successful, and they are justifiably proud of what they have accomplished.

LESSONS LEARNED FROM BALDWIN ELEMENTARY SCHOOL

Commitment by all staff to "do whatever it takes" to improve student achievement. The staff, teachers, and principal translate high expectations into a viable plan, embraced by all teachers and staff. That plan makes Baldwin one of the highest performing K–8 schools in Los Angeles.

Penetrating, relentless analysis of what is or is not working throughout the year. Ongoing revision of instruction occurs throughout the year to meet new challenges. This school uses the California Distinguished School rubric within its goals each year whether or not it is applying for Distinguished School designation.

Setting a higher bar for teachers, administration, and students. The Baldwin administration capitalizes on the strengths of teachers and staff and encourages all staff to perform at a higher level. All the standards are addressed, not just the essential ones.

"We take nothing for granted here," and *"We will continually strive to be excellent."*

7

Five Schools That Got the Job Done

Sustaining student achievement is on the minds of every school district and every administrator in our current high-stakes accountability environment. Everyone is looking for a "silver bullet" that will magically meet the ever-increasing demands of accountability requirements in No Child Left Behind (NCLB). It is also true that schools in areas with few perceived challenges cannot remain at "status quo" or "business as usual" levels in which the majority of students may be achieving. Schools across the nation must now shift from their emphasis on the majority to the minority of their students in significant subgroups where suddenly every single student must be accounted for. Furthermore, student achievement must now be sustained over time to keep pace with the expectations that are required in NCLB, when, in 2014, the student-achievement target will reach 100 percent proficiency.

Though some may scoff at the notion of actually reaching 100 percent, the truth is that the majority of schools are not even reaching 50 percent of their students performing proficiently. A looming wake-up call is coming down the line to schools that have been on cruise control, thinking that they will not have to address those hidden subgroups of students who are not achieving.

On the other hand, there exist a cadre of Title 1 schools that have confronted high poverty and large numbers of English learners and not only gotten the job of improving student achievement done but also discovered how to sustain that achievement. It would bode well for schools that have not had to pay attention to improving the achievement of all students to glean the principles and practices that have evolved from the day these schools had to face the hard truth that students were not achieving under their watch.

What are the secrets of these schools' successes? To attempt to answer this question, five Title 1 high-poverty, high-achieving elementary schools across the state of California that have extraordinarily sustained student achievement for a continuous five-year period or longer were studied. Woven within the story of each school are "magic" elements that have led to the sustaining of their achievement. The study did not attempt to capture these elements through a snapshot survey but rather by a case study methodology intended to illuminate each school's culture and practice. My aim was not merely to cite a listing of procedures and practices but to distill from each of the stories how the schools uniquely addressed the challenges faced and overcame what seemed to be daunting barriers. Each school successfully addressed student achievement and significantly closed the gap for significant subgroups, specifically English learners and the socioeconomically disadvantaged. What a success story to be told in public education!

What's more, each was found to have its unique focus based in its individual school context. Yet, what emerged was a set of common factors across the schools with five individual routes to success. A major finding was that each school began to initiate improvement in earnest when it reached a crisis point. Rather than submitting to failure, specific personalities emerged in key leadership roles to help each school make the systemic changes so necessary to sustaining success. For each of these five schools, the story began with a crisis that brought about change. This was certainly true of my own experience at Disney Elementary School.

A CRISIS POINT FORCES CHANGE

For each school, there came a moment in time when it was labeled low performing. At Disney, this moment came in 1999 when it was named an Immediate Intervention of Underperforming Schools Program (IIUSP) school, which was especially disheartening to teachers in place of being named a California Distinguished School two years earlier. Becoming an IIUSP school for Jefferson and Rosita was also their turning point in 1999. Teachers at Camellia Elementary School remember when their school was the worst performing school in the state in the 1970s. Baldwin teachers recall the pain of stalled and declining student achievement. Sylvan Elementary teachers still remember vividly the day they were labeled a challenge school in the district. Out of the response to the shock and pain of these hard places, improvement began to occur.

For any school, forced change spurred by accountability measures can be almost death dealing or certainly life producing. Schools are governed by cultures and traditions in "the way things are done." Teachers and principals become creatures of habit. Work with students becomes too automatic and unconscious. Too often what is done today is similar to what was done yesterday, whether or not it happens to generate results that are labeled as student achievement. A serious examination of student data that might indicate a need for improvement typically has not been a serious practice basic to the culture of schools.

I remember at Disney that we thought we were effective with students. After all, we had a highly renowned technology program, portfolio assessment system, and many other "pluses" to our school program. However, what we thought was effective proved to be mediocre at best. We had generalized and rationalized the real results of students and ignored one basic fact—our students, especially our English learners, could not read. For example, if our students were functioning at or about the fiftieth percentile on a standardized test, we generalized that our students were about what you would expect of a Title 1 school. Each student's individual performance data were not addressed. When standardized tests were given, we hoped for improvement rather than matching individual test results to actual names and faces associated with specific data.

How a school responds to change indicated by accountability measures will determine its individual success. Each of the five schools changed its practice to meet its student-achievement challenges. For each school, the change was systemic, transforming the culture within the school from a low-achieving culture to a high-achieving one. The changes were not easy for any of these schools, demanding a tremendous emotional, mental, and spiritual capacity to improve. Even today, changes associated with refinement continue to be hard work as each of these schools transforms to an even higher sustaining, achieving culture.

DEVELOPING A HIGH-ACHIEVING CULTURE

Sustained student achievement did not emanate from one practice or one policy but resulted from a combination of many specific beliefs, practices, and policies. Neither was the principal the key to the entire puzzle. It seems as if a high-achieving culture is a complex and unique blend of essential elements, with the blend depending on the school itself. Because the students of Camellia Elementary were so low performing and discipline was "out of control," teachers began with the strategies of classroom meetings and addressing student academic deficits. To this day, Camellia teachers will say, "Discipline is job number one." But the restoration of discipline and addressing academic deficits were only the beginning of establishing Camellia's high-achieving culture. Other essential elements were identified and subsequently incorporated over the years and continue to be evaluated as part of its culture.

For Jefferson Elementary, the principal and teachers began by emphasizing collaboration and teamwork as their primary emphasis in establishing their high-achieving culture. Both Sylvan Elementary and Baldwin Elementary were embarrassed by losing ground in their student-achievement scores. Principals at both schools recognized this and began to help teachers rebuild their self-esteem and pride in student achievement by focusing on high expectations and effective instruction. Sylvan teachers made quality instruction the centerpiece of their high-achieving culture. Again, this was only part of building a sustaining high-achieving culture. Rosita found itself as an IIUSP school and was forced to change. Rosita teachers and the principal began with grade-level meetings to help teachers work more effectively together to examine what was not working in instruction. Disney first focused on data in grade-level data meetings to identify key areas in instruction that were not adequately addressed, aligning them to the standards. For each school, the first area targeted for improvement has become a defining feature of its achieving culture. Further, as the high-achieving culture developed at each school, a set of core beliefs and a philosophy of high achieving also emerged.

NONNEGOTIABLE CORE VALUES

A very important part of sustaining each school's high-achieving culture is its core values and beliefs. Underlying each of these schools is a set of immutable core beliefs and values that ground the school's motivation and commitment to continue to succeed. I termed these *nonnegotiable core values.* The notion of nonnegotiable core values comes from the observations Carter (2000) made in high-performing schools articulated in his book *No Excuses*. Establishing the need for a core philosophy also comes from a wealth of effective schools literature on developing a shared vision (Blankstein, 2004; Marzano, 2003; Neuman & Simmons, 2000; Rosenholtz, 1991; among others). A predominant core value of high-achieving schools is that all children, even those from low-income or second-language backgrounds, can learn and become successful (Carter, 2000). High-achieving schools also embrace a collective accountability for all students and accept no excuses for failure. All five schools studied fervently believe that all of their children can and will learn.

Every high-achieving sustaining school has a core philosophy to which everyone in the school community subscribes. This belief system is so strong that when new teachers or staff members are employed at these schools, they must subscribe to the philosophy. Such is the case with Camellia Elementary School. New teachers are interviewed and queried about their willingness to live out their teaching careers at Camellia. One of Camellia's basic core values is that when you come to teach at Camellia, you will agree to remain a teacher. New teachers are also expected to teach the Camellia way that has proven to be successful. Within the culture, new teachers are not permitted to "do their own thing." Also, unique to Camellia's culture is that a principal is not permitted to "do his or her own thing" either apart from teachers.

At Rosita, two basic nonnegotiable core values direct all staff: "We believe that all students can achieve," and "We accept no less than 100 percent from everyone." Sylvan has three core beliefs: high expectations, no excuses, and ownership for instruction. For Jefferson, a nonnegotiable belief is that all staff will collaborate on instruction, use of data, staff development, and schoolwide responsibilities to improve student learning. Teachers are not allowed to opt out of faculty or grade-level meetings.

High expectations for students form the driving force behind Baldwin's core beliefs and success. High expectations are also central to forming the core motivation of the other four schools. New teachers coming into these schools are expected to conform to these beliefs. Both principals and teachers at all observed schools are quick to remind each other of their core beliefs continually through mottos and memos. Sylvan's principal occasionally refocuses teachers by putting a copy of the school's shared values in their mailboxes to help them continue to press forward when tough issues arise. These beliefs also remind them of the accountability they must feel to be successful and their commitment to sustain student achievement.

The achieving culture of all five schools is a unique-to-the-school blend of traditions, beliefs, and practices from both the past and the present. Each school has transformed student achievement from low achieving to high achieving. With that transformation came the travail of making many changes, the redefinition of core values, and the emergence and efficacy of new practices from past practices. The student success resultant from a high-achieving culture has given teachers a new swagger and a sense of pride in accomplishment. The transformation for each school was not easy and came from much blood, sweat, and tears. In some cases, teachers and administrators left the school in the middle of the transition. However, the practices and beliefs continued to be sustained by key leaders. What emerged at each of the schools were individuals who served as "keeper of the flame" to maintain the high-achieving culture. At Rosita, Sylvan, Baldwin, and Jefferson, the principal took on that role. Teachers also shared the role of keeper of the flame at the classroom level. At Camellia, specific leadership such as a veteran teacher or groups of teachers assumed that role. Regardless of the school, the high-achieving culture has been sustained and student learning continues to improve year upon year.

THE ESSENTIAL SUSTAINING ELEMENTS

An aspect of each school's high-achieving culture is a set of essential elements. All the schools had this in common. Though implemented and emphasized differently within each culture, these elements explain to some degree why these schools sustain. Each high-achieving culture has a core of five essential elements that, when taken singularly, are included in almost all effective schools literature of this era. All five schools did have these elements in common. However, it is important to note that these elements do not stand alone. They are built on each school's core values and integrated throughout the school. At each school, these elements take on varying degrees of importance, but all of the elements are present. The essential sustaining elements are high expectations for all students, shared leadership, good first teaching, use of student data, and strategic intervention for students.

High Expectations for All Students

Among schools across California, the banner of high expectations for all students may well have become a cliché, lacking the sustenance of truth. In all five schools, high expectations were tied to the prevailing belief that all students—including English learners, special education students, and other challenging groups—can achieve and do achieve. As a matter of fact, these schools made sure that students achieve. Rosita's principal told me, "Students don't have a choice—they are going to succeed." Over and over again, I heard, "We believe our students can do it!" Camellia teachers made a point of asking me to share with the readers of this book, "Our students can achieve and there are no ifs, ands, or buts about it!" This statement is verified by Camellia's high student achievement—among the elite in California. At Disney, we determined to "do everything possible, including carrying students across the finish line if we had to." This kind of commitment and determination combined with the proof that all students are achieving enabled teachers to become powerful and effective. Such efficacy is perpetuated through higher and higher expectations for students. What teachers once thought was impossible is now not good enough. So they do not settle; they continue to strive for higher achievement. Teachers no longer see student challenges as a barrier. Instead, they believe that their teaching will have a dramatic effect on student learning, and they are right.

Where each of these schools began with student achievement differs substantially from where they are today. In the beginning, each school had a majority of its students struggling specifically in reading and mathematics. When the schools first addressed student achievement, they had to concentrate all of their energies on helping students become competent in reading and mathematics. Because these schools have dramatically reduced the number of low-performing students who can't read, they now spend their time enriching the curriculum with the arts, history, and science. Jefferson, in its quest for greater achievement, did not abandon the arts and did make steady improvement in student achievement. Now all schools have the "luxury" of spending more time with students on developing important critical-thinking skills because basic reading and mathematics skills are in place. Student achievement continues to spiral higher and higher as the expectations of teachers consistently increase.

There is also a sense of pride and feelings of accomplishment in teachers at these schools. In low-achieving schools, when students are not successful, teachers tend to give up and not persevere with students. The lack of success breeds uncertainty and a prevailing belief that they cannot affect student achievement (Reksten, 1995). When teachers feel unsuccessful, even the more capable students in these schools do not achieve what is possible. Rosita teachers believed that, in the beginning, they did not have high enough expectations for students because of the barriers they saw with many English learners. At Disney, there came a point of deep despair when we looked at the true data of our students and wondered what more could we do. The stark reality of our students' reading deficits brought out every conceivable negative emotion. It was only when we implemented a plan with interim assessment as a centerpiece to measure the literacy skills of our students across the year that Disney teachers began to see changes in student achievement. Through the assessments, teachers saw how students were achieving—what was working and was missing in instruction. Once they committed themselves to addressing student deficits and began to see success, morale improved.

Sylvan teachers experienced the same frustration at the lack of success when they were labeled a challenge school. When they began to focus on effective instruction coordinated across the school, student achievement improved. Jefferson also experienced the pain when the school was labeled an underperforming school in 1999. Through collaboration and an emphasis on beginning reading skills, student achievement started to improve. All five schools transformed their lower expectations of students to higher expectations when they learned how to help students become successful.

Shared Leadership

The success of each of the five schools did not depend on just a few key individuals demonstrating leadership skills. Over time, the leadership for improving student achievement and learning in general was distributed to teachers and staff. Though the schools, for the most part, came to this major change in their own way, such a process has been advocated in the research. Distributing the leadership, according to Neuman and Simmons (2000), refers to reconceptualizing the leadership role from one or two leaders taking responsibility and authority to the entire school community taking responsibility and authority for leadership—especially leadership for student achievement. Neuman and Simmons further explain that the need for distributed leadership has developed from pressure within the past fifteen years to shift from traditional leadership roles of the principal or superintendent as a manager of daily school events to a schoolwide focus on student achievement. Educational leaders are now being asked to build strong cultures that foster collegial working, create a shared vision, articulate core values, develop collaborative decision making, and also manage the school. The principal as the sole leader of the school can no longer assume all of these responsibilities if schools are to ensure high-quality education for all students. Thus, leadership must be redistributed to share responsibilities across the school (Blankstein, 2004; Neuman & Simmons, 2000).

Empowering Teachers to Become Leaders

Empowering teachers to assume leadership roles in order to focus on student achievement was a priority at all schools. In four out of five schools, the principal was the main catalyst to develop and distribute leadership through a leadership team. Principals at Sylvan, Baldwin, Jefferson, and Rosita began by recreating each school's leadership team and refocusing it on student learning. Among all schools, teachers were allowed to select their representatives to the leadership team—usually from a grade level. The term of commitment on the leadership team was at least one year. With each of the four schools, staff development played an important role in early training of members to be leaders. At Rosita, leadership team meetings were highly structured by the principal, with that same structure replicated in the grade-level meeting, chaired by the grade-level leader. This same process occurred at Sylvan, Baldwin, and Jefferson. As matter of fact, these principals are now not even present at grade-level meetings so that grade-level leaders will lead the meetings. At Disney, teachers were encouraged to lead grade-level meetings. However, this was a difficult step in the beginning as teachers were not accustomed to shared leadership and decision making. The principal at Jefferson also indicated that teachers needed to be encouraged to take this important step. Setting the stage for sharing and distributing the leadership served to develop accountability for all students.

The agenda for leadership team meetings was developed by the principals at these four schools. However, each principal expected that the leadership team would participate in the discussion and problem solving. At these same schools, further clarification and refinement took place during grade-level meetings. The learning issues most commonly addressed included student interventions based on the most recent collection of data, implementation of instructional strategies, staff development triggered by data, scheduling issues, and other logistics problem solving—all directly pointed to student achievement. Recommendations from the leadership team meetings were then taken to grade levels for input. Then at faculty meetings, the entire school structure participated in this shared decision-making process.

At Camellia, the establishment of the leadership team originated from the teachers. The principal in the early 1970s did not stand in the way of teachers taking responsibility for student learning issues. She instead helped to facilitate the teachers' decisions. Teachers in the leadership team met to determine the academic plan and learning priorities of the school. Early priorities included establishing classroom meetings to control discipline and revamping instruction to "good first instruction." Camellia teachers coined the phrase, "If the student isn't learning, what did you teach first?" It is this fearless band of veteran teachers who have given their life to Camellia who continue to preserve the high-achieving culture, no matter what principal comes into the school. Each principal who has come to Camellia has been wise enough to preserve and enhance Camellia's achieving culture by staying out of the way of teachers and supporting their learning agendas.

A Commitment to Work Together

The commitment to work collaboratively is another important discovery that all schools made. It was not easy for any of these schools to collaborate with difficult personalities. But there was a growing understanding that working together could accomplish more than just a few teachers or administrators could. Now, each of these schools knows that working in isolation will not accomplish its goals. Teachers at these schools are not allowed to operate in isolation. At Jefferson Elementary, where collaboration is a significant part of their culture, the principal will insist that a teacher make up a meeting or training should he or she be absent. A wealth of research evidence supports this kind of collaborative working (Blankstein, 2004; Little, 1982; Lortie, 1975; Marzano, 2003; Rosenholtz, 1991; Schmoker, 2006; among others). The expectation at all five schools is that teachers will work together—there is no other option.

Further, they learned that the focus of their collaboration in the leadership team and grade-level meetings was not going to be on who will be supervising recess or other aspects of the school's operation. Instead these collaborative groups began examining the latest student data and comparing them to the essential standards and skills students should know so as to plan the next instructional unit. All staff members in each school came to feel a sense of urgency concerning student learning. As a result, a high level of professional dialogue developed on student learning issues across the school. This undoubtedly was an important essential element that led to their sustaining achievement.

Good First Teaching

The term *good first teaching* was used by Camellia to describe its expectation to teach well the first time so that students were successful immediately, thereby minimizing reteaching and the reinforcement of instructional errors. However, the phrase *good first teaching* originated with Madeline Hunter (2004) in *Mastery Teaching: Increasing Instructional Effectiveness in Elementary and Secondary Schools, Colleges and Universities*. This model consists of first identifying the teaching objective from the standards and curriculum material, task analyzing what needs to be taught first, demonstrating and modeling the skills and concepts within curriculum related to the teaching objective, guiding the practice of learners, providing feedback and/or correction to the learner followed by a summary of and/or assessment of what was learned, and independent practice. At Sylvan Elementary, this model is stressed with all teachers. As a matter of fact, this teaching model is standardized across the school so that there is continuity of instruction.

At all schools, there is a focus on essential standards and student mastery of these standards. The grade-level teams in each of these schools have identified essential standards—those frequently assessed that students must master. As a means of checking mastery, students are frequently assessed and instruction is monitored and adjusted to reteach or accelerate when necessary. Additionally, a process is in place to plan and continually align the essential standards to curriculum-based materials so that instruction is targeted and focused. Even though all schools use approved, standards-based curricula, the curricula are not 100 percent aligned to the California standards. There is an understanding that the school needs to adjust the curriculum to better address the standards in some cases. These schools do not automatically assume every page of the standards-based curriculum fully supports essential standards. Neither do they try to teach every page of the standards-aligned curriculum. They understand that grade-level teams must constantly make adjustments within the curriculum based on the standards and on student assessment results.

The idea that each teacher has the option to determine what he or she teaches is nonexistent at these schools. Instruction must be choreographed so that all students receive a coherent and explicit curriculum across all grades. Grade-level teams serve an important purpose in coordinating the classroom instruction to the end that students achieve grade-level standards and beyond. At all schools, instruction was coordinated through the grade levels. At Camellia, teachers new to the staff were expected to teach like other teachers at Camellia. At Sylvan, the principal orients new teachers to the Madeline Hunter model and makes sure these teachers are effective immediately. At Baldwin, the Title 1 Curriculum Specialist works very closely with new teachers to assist them in implementing grade-level curriculum. At Jefferson, every teacher is expected to embrace the collaborative decisions regarding implementing specific instructional strategies within the curriculum. Overall, good first teaching is planned, targeted, and coordinated at each school so that students are continually mastering the standards.

Use of Student Data

The use of student data is vital to the continuing quest for sustained student achievement at all the schools. All schools begin the school year with a review of STAR data to identify strengths and weaknesses in the instructional program and to set priorities for the year. Baldwin spent a great deal of time using the state data (which they termed an "accountability review") to not only set priorities for the school but for each grade level during the first two months of the school year. Student data from the STAR tests called out the strengths and weaknesses in the instructional program. For each of the five schools, this information helped to set priorities across the school year. Additionally, every school examined the performance level of each student—Advanced, Proficient, Basic, Below Basic, and Far Below Basic—from the California Standards Tests (CSTs). Grade-level teams used the performance score of each student for grouping students within the classroom to intervene or accelerate learning.

By far, the most important data collected across the year are benchmark assessment data. Every school has determined a set of assessments and organized a system for collecting those assessments, common across the school. The types of benchmark assessments used are formative, as in the beginning stages of reading in kindergarten and first grade where decoding skills are assessed, or summative in checking the comprehension of grade-level concepts found in the standards. Diagnostic assessments are used primarily to determine what reading or math skills are missing. The chief purpose of these assessments is to measure each student's learning across the year. In fact, all schools monitored each student individually. Baldwin Elementary developed a prescribed learning plan for each student that was carefully monitored.

Leadership teams and grade levels play an important role in interpreting the assessment data collected on students. It is one thing to collect the data and quite another to analyze them to determine the next steps with students. Camellia and Sylvan teachers met in grade levels and reviewed student data from the Sacramento County Office of Education (SCOE) *Reading First Assessments* every six weeks. Both of these schools reviewed the assessment results student by student and then acted on the data through intervention in the classrooms. One of the most important steps at Disney Elementary was establishing a process for analyzing student assessment data and determining how that data would be used to improve achievement. At Disney, we felt that teachers must develop a good understanding of the targets for reading skills found within the standards as a first priority. All five schools also understood the importance of monitoring the formation of reading skills. For example, Disney teachers know that students in Grade 1 must finish the grade-level reading of at least sixty words per minute (WPM) to be ready for Grade 2 reading standards. At all schools, when assessments were collected, teachers met in grade levels and distinguished student by student those who achieved proficiency from those who were not proficient with grade-level standards.

A process was in place at each school for examining benchmark data from student assessments. The important finding among all the schools is that teachers are quick to adjust their instruction based on a pattern they see in student data. Schools that do not use student data are not making the adjustments they need to make as indicated by the data. And if teachers are not working collaboratively, they will not see the changes they need to make across the school to benefit all students. Once these schools saw a pattern with data and problems with certain students, they intervened quickly and decisively. These schools were simply not going to let their students fail. Because they have been so effective in eliminating the large number of students who were struggling with reading, higher and higher targets for benchmark assessments are now being set.

Strategic Intervention for Students

At all five schools, achievement was monitored student by student. At Rosita and Jefferson, the principal met with each teacher three times during the year to review individual student data. Discussions focused on each student's achievement and how the teacher planned to address reteaching, grouping, and/or interventions. At Sylvan, teachers met twice each year in "cooperatives" consisting of the resource specialist teacher, principal, learning facilitator, and school psychologist to review the progress of each student. Within Disney's grade-level team meetings, students who were not performing were listed on "the roll call" to determine the best course of action to address student deficits. Jefferson teachers posted student data on the "data wall" in the staff room to communicate student performance to all staff. Rosita teachers monitored students each week, intervening if students fell behind. At all schools, the collaborative structures and data monitoring systems helped teachers find solutions for complex problems related to learning issues they saw among students at the grade levels.

Once teachers pinpoint each student's difficulty, the right intervention must be selected. If students are placed haphazardly in interventions without a diagnosis, they will not improve in achievement. All five schools carefully identified through assessments what the specific reading and mathematics issues were. Students were then carefully placed within intervention programs that specifically matched their learning needs. For example, at Camellia, students weak in comprehension were grouped within Open Court's "workshop time" to work on comprehension skills. At Sylvan, students were scheduled based on need into specific interventions during "Universal Access" time. Every school had a system for matching the student's learning needs to the correct intervention.

Analysis of benchmark assessment data throughout the year determines which students will be identified for strategic intervention at all five schools. The first level of intervention is always within the classroom. Within grade-level teams, teachers discussed and determined how they would intervene with students. For Sylvan, a highly organized time called Universal Access, taken from the Houghton Mifflin reading series, is used strategically across the school to intervene and to accelerate learning. At Jefferson, students were regrouped based on specific reading or math needs within the school day, after school, or on Saturdays. Camellia hired an instructional assistant for each classroom to specifically work with teachers to intervene with struggling students. Baldwin uses a schoolwide strategy to group English learners within the school day to assist them with language development. During principal meetings with teachers, students were selected for after-school intervention based on reading needs (e.g., fluency, comprehension). All schools recognized that (1) the classroom is the first safety net for intervening with struggling students and (2) leadership team and grade-level collaboration assist these schools with more complex grouping involving more than one grade level. Teaming proved to be an important strategy for intervention.

A second approach to intervention with students occurs through extended day formats. Sylvan, Jefferson, Rosita, and Baldwin incorporated these formats to work more intensively with students beyond the school day. Saturdays are scheduled for intervention classes at Jefferson. Baldwin has an extensive homework program and intervention program after school. At Disney, we found that our Power Reading classes prior to the school day were effective with students, especially when students received the correct intervention.

Rosita developed a unique program of academic contracts with students and parents that combined personal responsibility with intervention. Academic contracts were based on the school's Title 1 home-school compact signed by students, parents, and teachers. Within the compact, students agree to come to school with a positive attitude, work hard in class, complete homework, follow school rules, and commit to daily reading practice. Students experiencing difficulty in any one of the five areas were recommended for an academic contract. The principal and teacher take responsibility for meeting with the parent and monitoring the student weekly toward completing the contract. When the student satisfied the contract, there was a big celebration for that student. What is unique about this is that this approach deals with the whole child, not just intervening with his or her reading or math issues. The principal and teachers monitored these contracts religiously. Academic contracts are a big reason why Rosita, with the largest number of English learners among the five schools, is sustaining student achievement.

In summary, each school staff spent time checking, rechecking, and checking again using assessment and intervention. They have learned to make adjustments quickly and to intervene because they know the academic needs of students so well. Everyone understands the mission of student achievement at each school—not just teachers and administrators. Classified staff members understood their role of supporting teachers and the mission of the school. Instructional assistants were trained to administer assessments and work alongside teachers in the classroom. Students participated in monitoring their own achievement at all schools through goal setting. Every school that is sustaining continues to learn and grow toward higher and higher student achievement to make sure that no student is left behind.

A FINAL WORD

Essential elements emerged and were discovered that have enabled these schools to be sustaining through the high-achieving culture that has been created. It is important to note that these essential elements do not operate in isolation but within a school's high-achieving culture and the personalities that make that culture unique. There is no doubt that developing a high-achieving culture is complex and takes great effort especially where the school is low achieving. However, the important point is that *any* school can become high achieving, as shown from the five schools profiled in this book. Camellia was at the bottom of the list of schools in California during the 1970s and now it is at the top of the list of achieving schools in the state.

Another important finding is that there are many routes to becoming a sustaining school. Each school had its unique focus and emphasis and yet still became high achieving as long as the essential elements were integral to that high-achieving culture.

Furthermore, the principal is not necessarily the key to a sustaining culture. To build a sustaining school, it takes everyone, not just the principal, to make extraordinary gains in achievement. The answer lies in all the collective personalities that make up the school, working collaboratively and together living out the school's core values—believing all children can learn and making it happen.

What is remarkable is that each school marched to its own drum and yet arrived at exactly the same place as the other schools—sustained student achievement. Every school experienced tremendous emotional struggle to get the improvement process started. There are vivid recollections of the pain and challenge. However, that pain and challenge have now been replaced by great pride and joy of accomplishment in the work that's been done. In the beginning, it seemed overwhelming to address the student learning challenges with which the schools were confronted. Some teachers couldn't take the emotional challenge and bailed out. Others rose up and accepted the challenge and made student achievement happen.

The new level of success they have obtained has prompted these schools to take on even greater challenges. They have taken the stance that "Nothing is too difficult for us" and "Bring it on" because "We will get it done." Camellia's prior principal used to say, "When you are successful, it doesn't seem like work." Each school's success has brought a thirst for even greater achievement and propelled it into a continuous cycle of greater and greater improvement. For many teachers, this has become their life's work. Their work is validated by the accomplishments of their students. There is so much to learn from these schools. They have achieved the impossible with the greatest of challenges, and they continue to achieve more. These are the stories of a sustaining school.

References

Blankstein, A. M. (2004). *Failure is not an option*. Thousand Oaks, CA: Corwin Press.

Brewster, C., & Fager, J. (2000). *Increasing student engagement and motivation: From time-on-task to homework*. Portland, OR: Northwest Regional Educational Laboratory.

Buly, M. R., & Valencia, S. (2003, April). *Meeting the needs of failing readers: Cautions and considerations for state policy*. State policy paper, Center for the Study of Teaching and Policy, University of Washington.

Carter, S. C. (2000). *No excuses*. Washington, DC: The Heritage Foundation.

Cunningham, P. M., & Allington, R. L. (2006). *Classrooms that work*. Upper Saddle River, NJ: Pearson.

Diamond, L. (2007). *CORE teaching reading sourcebook* (2nd ed.). Novato, CA: Arena.

Doyle, M. (1976). *How to make meetings work*. New York: Berkley.

Dreikurs, R., & Cassell, P. (1991). *Discipline without tears: A reassuring and practical guide to teaching your child positive behavior* (2nd ed.). New York: Plume.

Engelmann, S. (1980). *Direct instruction*. Englewood Cliffs, NJ: Educational Technology Publications.

Hunter, M. (2004). *Mastery teaching: Increasing instructional effectiveness in elementary and secondary schools, colleges and universities* (2nd ed.). Thousand Oaks, CA: Corwin Press.

Little, J. (1982). Norms of collegiality and experimentation: Workplace conditions of school success. *American Educational Research Journal 19*, 325–340.

Lortie, D. C. (1975). *School teacher: A sociological study*. Chicago: University of Chicago Press.

Marzano, R. J. (2003). *What works in schools*. Alexandria, VA: Association for Supervision and Curriculum Development (ASCD).

McPeak, L. (2000). *Core elements of instruction*. Modesto, CA: Stanislaus Office of Education to the Consortium of Underperforming Schools.

Neuman, M., & Simmons, W. (2000). Leadership for student learning. *Phi Delta Kappan, 82*(1), 9–12.

Reksten, L. E. (1995). *Teacher efficacy and the school context*. UCLA Dissertation Abstracts, 1995.

Rosenholtz, S. J. (1991). *Teachers' workplace*. New York: Teachers College Press.

Schmoker, M. J. (2006). *Results now: How we can achieve unprecedented improvement in teaching and learning*. Alexandria, VA: Association for Supervision and Curriculum Development (ASCD).

Index

CORWIN PRESS

The Corwin Press logo—a raven striding across an open book—represents the union of courage and learning. Corwin Press is committed to improving education for all learners by publishing books and other professional development resources for those serving the field of PreK–12 education. By providing practical, hands-on materials, Corwin Press continues to carry out the promise of its motto: **"Helping Educators Do Their Work Better."**